Waiting for God, Justice, and Rush-Hour Traffic

Waiting for God, Justice, and Rush-Hour Traffic

The Creative Activity of Patience

Dennis Okholm

CASCADE *Books* · Eugene, Oregon

WAITING FOR GOD, JUSTICE, AND RUSH-HOUR TRAFFIC
The Creative Activity of Patience

Cascade Books
An Imprint of Wipf and Stock Publishers
199 W. 8th Ave., Suite 3
Eugene, OR 97401

www.wipfandstock.com

PAPERBACK ISBN: 979-8-3852-1369-6
HARDCOVER ISBN: 979-8-3852-1370-2
EBOOK ISBN: 979-8-3852-1371-9

Cataloguing-in-Publication data:

Names: Okholm, Dennis, author.

Title: Waiting for God, justice, and rush-hour traffic : the creative activity of patience / Dennis Okholm.

Description: Eugene, OR: Cascade Books, 2025. Includes bibliographical references.

Identifiers: ISBN 979-8-3852-1369-6 (paperback) | ISBN 979-8-3852-1370-2 (hardcover) | ISBN 979-8-3852-1371-9 (ebook)

Subjects: LCSH: Patience—Religious aspects—Christianity. | Christian life. | Benedictines—Spiritual life.

Classification: BV4647.P3 O3 2025 (paperback) | BV4647.P3 (ebook)

VERSION NUMBER 06/10/25

To Trevecca,
the partner and friend who has been patient with me
for more than fifty years

Contents

A Prefatory Warning
of What's Ahead

A WARNING IS APPROPRIATE: reader beware! Reading this book
will require patience. We've been aware of this kind of thing for a
long time. In the third century Cyprian began his treatise on patience with this bit of advice: "I see that even at this time, for your
audience of me, patience is needful, as you cannot even discharge
this duty of hearing and learning without patience. For wholesome
discourse and reasoning are then effectually learnt, *if* what is said
be patiently heard."[1] In other words, reading this book—a book
with footnotes no less—will itself be training in patience.

To the point, perhaps it is lack of patience that accounts for
the fact that a quarter of adults in the US have not read a book
in whole or in part in recent years.[2] Statistics like that reinforce

1. Cyprian, "Patience," 1. Cyprian might have had a bedfellow in the twen-
tieth century with the likes of Jacques Ellul in his diatribes against what he
called "technique." Of the books written in the sixteenth and seventeenth centuries he observed that they "were not written to be used . . . to locate a piece of
information accurately and quickly, or to validate or invalidate an experiment,
or to furnish a formula. They were not written to be consulted. They were
written to be read patiently in their entirety and to be mediated upon." (Ellul,
Technological Society, 40). The present book is written in that spirit. Though,
because it would take a bit more patience than is necessary, note that some
quotations taken from the *Ante-Nicene Fathers and Nicene and Post-Nicene
Fathers* series will be paraphrased.

2. Gelles-Watnick and Perrin, "Who Doesn't Read?," lines 1–3.

Alan Kreider's claim in his nuanced narrative of the early church: "Patience is unconventional: It reconfigures behavior according to Jesus' teachings in many areas, especially wealth, sex, and power."[3]

Granted that it doesn't have much to do with wealth, sex, and power, but my experience on Los Angeles freeways confirms Kreider's claim. In fact, examples of impatience show up in the course of everyday life because we are temporal creatures. I recently experienced it on the phone waiting to speak to a human being while the business offered their recorded explanation: "All our representatives are currently handling other calls. Please continue to hold for the next available representative. Thank you for your *patience*." This was repeated every thirty seconds for a half-hour. This confirmed David Fagerberg's observation that cultivating endurance "requires the passage of time. Who else but a temporal creature can develop the virtue of patience?"[4]

Yet, the virtue of patience is not only *not* developed among most temporal creatures today; it has largely been *ignored* in the field of Christian ethics. Such is the claim of Stanley Hauerwas and Charles Pinches:

> We moderns fill our lives with what Albert Borgmann characterizes as a kind of addiction to hyperactivity. Believing that we live in a world of infinite possibilities, we find ourselves constantly striving, restless for what, we are not sure. We call our restlessness freedom, but more often than not our freedom seems more like fate, especially when we get what we have strived for only to discover that it does not satisfy.[5]

This restlessness and impatience become habitual, as Tish Harrison Warren admitted when she wrote, "In my daily life I've developed habits of impatience—of speeding ahead, of trying to squeeze more into my cluttered day. How can I live as one who

---

3. Kreider, *Patient Ferment*, 55.
4. Fagenberg, "Time in the Desert Fathers," 182.
5. Hauerwas and Pinches, "Practicing Patience," 175.

watches and waits for the coming kingdom when I can barely wait for water to boil?"[6]

My wife exhorted me to have patience while we backpacked across Catalina Island. The exhortation included a warning: "If you don't wait for me, I'm not going any farther!" I waited. It turned out to be five days cultivating this virtue.

But there are so many other opportunities to cultivate patience: waiting for a lab report; inexplicable lag time on the computer or internet; being forced to use snail mail rather than email; anticipating the descent of a lobbed tennis ball before smashing it over the net; seeking quick answers that cannot be found to some daily household problems; exercising caution in daily life until a vaccine is found for a pandemic; praying incessantly for a friend to become a disciple of Jesus; struggling to achieve justice for abuse that was suffered. We will discover along the way that such cultivated patience is not acquiescence; it is creatively active.

So patience is not to be underestimated. Waiting is a pervasive theme in our lives. We all are waiting for something. Helmut Thielicke reminds me of this in a sermon he preached last century:

> Our entire life is one single "waiting." As children we wait until we will become grown-ups. . . . Then we wait for the end of our education, for the first self-earned money, then for our life's companion, then for children, and after that for the time when the children will be grown and on their own. So it goes on and on. And when we have nothing more to wait for, that is death—by no means because the end of our professional life, all of our productive functions, and ultimately our physical death await us. No, where waiting ends, that is the end of life itself.[7]

We wait for rush-hour traffic. We wait for justice. We even wait for God. All of it requires the virtue of patience. The importance of this virtue in our lives becomes apparent when we survey the damage done by *im*patience. And so we begin.

---

6. Warren, *Liturgy of the Ordinary*, 104.

7. Thielicke, *How to Hope Again*, 172.

I

Impatience

The Cause of Humanity's Downfall and of Every Sin

LIKE ITS COUSIN HUMILITY, the virtue of patience was a distinctively *Christian* virtue in the Western philosophical world at the time early Christian theologians wrote treatises on it. Tertullian, Cyprian, John Cassian, and Augustine all wrote extensively on the topic. Plato, Cicero, and Seneca wrote about the virtue of *endurance* in the face of adversity, but they did not unpack *patience* as did these early Christian theologians.[1] For one thing, as a Christian virtue, patience was not focused on the self—one's own interests, as Greek humanism held. It was focused on the service of others (Col 3:13) and was typically expected in reciprocal relationships (Eph 4:2).[2] Relatedly, in the New Testament, patience is often found in

1. Wilken, *Early Christian Thought*, 283.

2. See Falkenroth and Brown, "Patience," 765–66. Donato Ogliari points out that the Greco-Roman tradition, influenced by the advent of Stoicism, conceived of patience as a virtue that enabled the wise person to remain invulnerable to life's risks and trials. But such was achieved by personal effort that reduced patience to a "secularized ethic, essentially self-control, preoccupied with the present state of things and cooly based on reason and will"; this, over against Christian patience that is rooted in the patience of God and that mainly relies on God and is open to the future promised by God's Son. See

1

context with kindness and hospitality (e.g., Gal 5:22) and as a way of life that expresses love (1 Cor 13:4). In fact, it is *impatience* that is linked with self-interest in the biblical story.

It was Tertullian and Cyprian who credited the devil with the authorship of impatience. "Impatience is the mischief of the devil," Cyprian writes. "The devil suffered with impatience because man was made in the image of God. Hence he was the first to perish and to ruin others"—namely, Adam, Cain, Esau, and Israel. But Cyprian did not stop there: "Moreover, impatience makes heretics in the Church."[3] After all, it took the early church three hundred years, carefully working its way through well-intentioned heresies that often took the easy way out, just to come up with a decent statement that clarified how Christians can insist that they worship one God who is three persons at the same time.

Cyprian concedes that Adam's fall left all of us to live in sorrow and groaning, sweat and toil, tribulations and mischiefs of the devil, persecutions and imprisonments "to be endured in the faith and courage of patience." Cyprian hopes that we will learn from this: "if we who have renounced the devil and the world with more frequency and violence, how much more ought we to keep patience, wherewith as our helper and ally, we may bear all mischievous things!"[4]

Tertullian offers *his* explanation how this all entered the human race, chauvinistically laying much of the blame on Eve. Grieving over God's choice to assign the Creator's image to humans, just as Cyprian had said, the devil's envy prompted him to deceive Eve. Malice became both the cause and the result of the impatience that drove the devil to transmit the same impatience to his victim. So the woman was then "breathed on by a spirit infected with impatience" and would not have sinned if she had maintained patience to the end, obeying God, resisting the devil's ploys, and waiting for her husband (a point of view as sexist to modern ears as the opposite scenario described in Brad Paisley's song, "Waitin' on a

Ogliari, "*Laus Patientiae*," 7.

3. Cyprian, "Patience," 19.

4. Cyprian, "Patience," 10–12.

Woman"). In a chain of events, Eve's impatience imperils "another human being"—Adam—who will eventually die due to his own impatience, by means of which he himself perishes. But, though humans become easily turned by impatience, Tertullian observes that the first time God got angry was also the first time God exercised patience. And so we see a contrast by the time we get to the third chapter of Genesis—a contrast that will be replicated throughout the biblical story: divine patience bears mercy, while human impatience becomes "the womb to every delinquency." As far as Tertullian is concerned, "every sin is ascribable to impatience . . . evil is impatience of good."[5] Or, as Blaise Pascal put it, "I have discovered that all human evil comes from this—man's being unable to sit still in a room."[6]

To illustrate, Tertullian elaborates on the notion that adultery is committed through the impatience of lust. This is true not just on a human level. Tertullian sees it exemplified in the Old Testament by Israel's adulterous acts toward Yahweh when Aaron does not wait for Moses to come down from the mountain (Exod 32:1) or when Israel complained for lack of water at Meribah (Num 20:1–13) or the times they harmed the prophets. "Had they entered the path of patience, they would have been set free," a point that would be drilled into them whenever they cited Psalm 95 that recalled their hardened hearts at Meribah, prompting the Lord's anger to affirm, "They shall never enter my rest."[7] The point is drilled into us every Friday morning during the Lenten daily lectionary reading of the same psalm.

If every sin is attributable to impatience, perhaps Tertullian's discussion of its relation to revenge is the most poignant, especially for us who live in a world of clashing cultures, religious and political ideologies, and competing empires that have the nuclear capability to bounce the rubble. From the world's perspective, Tertullian observes that revenge is thought to be the healer of pain, when, in truth, it is deadly. One who knew that truth, Nelson

---

5. Tertullian, "Patience," 3, 5.

6. Pascal, *Pensees*, 139 (paraphrased).

7. Tertullian, "Patience," 3, 5.

Mandela, comes to mind as Tertullian rewords Romans 12:19: "Leave patience to me, and I will reward patience." Though Mandela was not coming at life from a strictly Christian perspective, his story is perhaps the most remarkable contemporary illustration of the creative activity of patience that refuses to engage in vengeful anger. If he had responded to injustice differently than he had responded, he would have confirmed what our early church fathers said about the all-pervasive damage in human lives that is attributable to impatience.

At the age of seventy-one, Mandela was released from prison in February 1990, having spent over ten thousand days in jail since his initial arrest for treason in 1963—a jail term that he expected to last for five years at most.[8] After the first six months on Robben Island (comparable to Alcatraz), he was transported back to Pretoria, standing in the hold of an old boat below a porthole through which workers urinated on him. Found guilty of sabotage, a verdict for which he took responsibility, he was given a life sentence. Mandela would later reflect, "There is nothing like a long spell in prison to focus your mind and to bring you to a more sober appreciation of the realities of your society."[9]

Prison forced him to think more deeply about his principles and ideals, to stand back and see himself as others saw him, to learn to control his temper and strong will, to empathize and persuade and extend his influence over other prisoners and warders. He was returned to Robben Island, his home for the next eighteen years, beginning with an eight-foot-by-seven-foot cell, a straw mat, and three threadbare blankets. He later said, "You have no idea of the cruelty of man against man until you have been in a South African prison with white warders and black prisoners."[10] But throughout he did not compromise his ideals and maintained hope.

He would respect warders as human beings, combined with pity rather than hatred, recognizing the insecurities and psychological deformities of the warders. Those who had seen his temper

8. What follows is taken from Sampson, *Mandela*.
9. Sampson, *Mandela*, 343.
10. Sampson, *Mandela*, 203.

in the past were amazed how he was able to restrain himself in the most humiliating circumstances.[11] The new head of the prison, who made Robben more humane, said of Mandela, "I never felt he was *waiting* for revenge."[12] Instead, Mandela's waiting—his patience—was exhibited in discussions with warders whom he sought to educate about apartheid and race, in his own self-education of the Afrikaner mindset and language, understanding the indoctrination that led to the inability to see the black man as a human being. And just as the devil's malicious impatience infected the first humans in the Genesis story, so Mandela's patient response to his warders was infectious. One previously militant prisoner who had been brutally tortured observed Mandela's calm, his refusal to display bitterness without compromise, his ability to laugh at the brutality, and his conviction that those who tortured were lesser human beings. As a result he concluded, "I came out [of prison] a different person. . . . I think I am a relatively calm person now."[13] And another prisoner who observed Mandela's strong character said, "He gave us hope when everything was rock bottom and we saw no future."[14]

His biographer, Anthony Sampson, reflects on all of this by saying, "Mandela's forgiveness was shared by many of his fellow prisoners, who were determined to avoid bitterness and self-pity. . . . his deeper understanding of human courage, suffering and sacrifice reassured the prisoners that they were part of a universal drama."[15] His contemporaries developed self-control and tolerance, but Mandela was the chief role model, while still radiating authority and refusing to be a sellout. Making the point that "the prison graduates would retain much of the same spirit after they left prison," Sampson quotes one fellow prisoner, "I can spot a Robben Islander a mile away. When they find themselves in a conflict, they have the containment of anger, which is then

---

11. See Sampson, *Mandela*, 213–22.
12. Sampson, *Mandela*, 224, emphasis added.
13. Sampson, *Mandela*, 226.
14. Sampson, *Mandela*, 230.
15. Sampson, *Mandela*, 230–31.

channeled. I'm really thankful for it. It has had quite an impact on conflict situations, including my home life."[16]

Mandela saw the prisoners' garden as a metaphor of the political leader who "sows seeds, and then watches, cultivates and harvests the results."[17] With such patience Mandela developed control over his anger, and with a determined but kind and gentle manner he was able to suppress his emotions in order to think clearly in the worst circumstances.[18]

Controlling anger was not accompanied by acquiescence. He still had a streak of rebelliousness and independence such that, at one point, he joined a hunger strike for six weeks that led to a negotiated settlement that allowed children as young as three to visit the island.[19]

With violence escalating, and with world leaders such as Prime Minister Margaret Thatcher and President Ronald Reagan considering Mandela and the ANC (African National Congress) to be Communist terrorists, South African Prime Minister Botha offered Mandela his release if he renounced violence. But Mandela refused and insisted it was Botha who must renounce violence and dismantle apartheid before Mandela would accept his freedom. They even tried to acclimate Mandela to freedom and compromise himself with occasional excursions from prison, but, as Sampson says, "he was prepared to *wait*."[20] Though he could not accept the conditions for his release and remained loyal to the ANC, he continued with diplomacy and negotiations with the government until he was the only major opposition leader in prison. Finally, Prime Minister deKlerk reversed most of the policies of his predecessors over the past thirty years, and Mandela walked out of prison on February 11, 1990.

---

16. Sampson, *Mandela*, 289–90.

17. Sampson, *Mandela*, 237, 242.

18. Sampson, *Mandela*, 233, 237, 242.

19. Sampson, *Mandela*, 283.

20. See Sampson, *Mandela*, 330–50, and for quotation, 348, emphasis added.

Impatience

Not trapped in the past and as the personification of the future, Sampson says, Mandela's "magnanimity and lack of bitterness conveyed a moral seriousness, particularly to white South Africans, as if he were a priest at confessional, forgiving sins and giving his blessing." He goes on to say,

> Mandela's basic appeal was not as a man of power, but as a moral leader who had stood out for fundamental principles and who gave hope for the future to all oppressed people and all countries torn by racial divisions. His dignity and wish for reconciliation gave him an influence beyond ordinary politics. . . . Certainly Mandela had an overoptimistic view of the struggle before he went to jail in 1962; but his prison ordeal transformed him into a much more reflective and influential kind of leader. . . . He learned about human sensitivities and how to handle the fears and insecurities of others, including his Afrikaner warders. He was sensitized by his own sense of guilt, both about his family and about friends he had used during his political career; but he was acquiring a deeper confidence, feeling himself "master of my fate," like a classical hero. Unlike most politicians, in midcareer he had time to become much more thoughtful and questioning, reading biographies and histories. And he deepened his interest in the law, which, though it had put him in jail, he realized provided the only basis for a lasting settlement: the law, not war, was the basis of his hopes for his country's future.[21]

As he had watched the South African stage as a spectator, Mandela's unpublished essays and writings from jail showed far more intellectual depth and originality than his early anti-colonialist clichés; and he was persistent in getting to the truth, however uncomfortable.

> The fortitude and resilience of the Robben Island prisoners were a communal achievement, and Mandela might not have maintained his strength without his colleagues. . . . But in the end his personal leadership was

---

21. Sampson, *Mandela*, 405.

> decisive. . . . without Mandela South African history
> would have taken a completely different turn. His con-
> ciliation emerged from his personal development: he had
> learned how to control his aggression, to "think with his
> brains, not his blood," and to channel his energy into the
> goal of a negotiated victory. He became a much more
> formidable politician by subordinating his emotions and
> feelings to his central purpose. . . . He had been "steeled
> and hardened," . . . and his underlying toughness was es-
> sential to the success of the negotiations which followed.[22]

Without ignoring or minimizing the injustice Mandela recognized and suffered, his example stands out as a testimony to the
creative activity of the virtue of patience that finds outlets leading
to a just reconciliation rather than vengeful anger that would only
make things worse.

Mandela's life exemplifies Tertullian's recognition that patience is necessary to forgive seven times seventy, but the impatient
cannot forgive even once. Tertullian concludes that the vengeance
motivated by impatience leads to all kinds of evil; he will have none
of it: "What have I to do with vengeance, the measure of which,
through impatience of pain, I am unable to regulate? Whereas, if I
shall repose in patience, I shall not *feel* pain; if I shall not feel pain,
I shall not *desire* to avenge myself."[23] This connection between
patience and revenge will take on added significance when we
consider the church's mission in the next chapter.

Of course, even in cases of revenge there can be a kind of
counterfeit patience, something John Cassian discusses in his

22. Sampson, *Mandela*, 415, 573–74.

23. Tertullian, "Patience," 10, 12. Gregory the Great, first great pope of the
church, said something similar when he observed that the impatient commit
acts they did not intend because "impetuosity drives the mind whither it does
not wish. In its agitated state it acts as if it did not know what it was doing, only
to feel regret when later it realizes what it has done." Such folks "sometimes
act as if they were other than they are, and hardly recognize the evil they have
done. . . . they upset the good they may have done when the mind was tranquil,
and by their sudden impulse they undo what with protracted labor they have
built up. . . . The less patient a man proves to be, the less instructed does he
show himself to be." Gregory, *Pastoral Care*, 107.

conference "On Friendship."[24] A feigned patience may arouse even more anger in the other person than would a vengeful word that is spoken: "a spiteful silence surpasses the harshest verbal abuse." Cassian is wise when he observes that we sometimes convince ourselves that we are patient when we respond to an irritated person with a "bitter silence or by a ridiculing movement or gesture in such a way that we provoke them to anger more by our silent response than we would have been able to incite them by passionate abuse. And in this way we consider ourselves blameless before God, since we have said nothing that could brand or condemn us according to the judgment of human beings."

Most married people can identify with the description of one who imagines he is the paragon of virtue when he responds to his partner in a sullen silence with suppressed impatience that really only exacerbates problems and essentially mocks the other person.

Tertullian recognizes bogus patience among the rich and those who give invitations to the rich.[25] In other words, he was suggesting that it is easy to "endure" when one has abundant resources, and it is not really patience that is operative when one puts up with abuse at the hands of the well-to-do simply because he is hoping to gain some advantage from them down the pike.

Cyprian also cited what *seems* to be patience among the philosophers who expounded on the topic without knowing the wisdom or patience of God.[26] But it was Augustine who argued that it is the difference in *motivation and goal* of what *appears* to be patience that belies its genuineness. He argued that we should neither praise nor imitate those who exercise patience for reasons that are not virtuous, since "it transfers the characteristics of this virtue of patience to vices. For instance, patience is the companion of wisdom, not the handmaiden of immoral desires. Patience is the friend of a good conscience, not the enemy of innocence. . . . So when you see anyone patiently enduring some suffering, don't immediately

---

24. See Cassian, *Conferences*, 16:18 (paraphrased) for what follows.
25. Tertullian, "Patience," 16.
26. Cyprian, "Patience," 2.

praise it as patience, because patience has to do with *cause* of the suffering. When it is a good cause, then it is truly patience."[27]

It is not only the ancients who understood the severity of impatience in the history of human relationships. Michael Casey makes the same point: "Patience is our most accessible means of living the way Christ lived. We rarely include its opposite in our list of negative behaviors, yet chronic impatience destroys both our sense of self-worth and our communion with those around us. Franz Kafka once wrote in *Aphorisms*, 'Impatience got people evicted from Paradise . . . and impatience kept them from making their way back.' That makes failures in patience pretty serious."[28]

Stanley Hauerwas and Charles Pinches put it bluntly: "impatience is a crucial sin that carries us into other sins." And this makes their assessment of the current state of Christian ethics even more profound when, as we mentioned in the preface, they claim that "the virtue of patience has especially been ignored."[29] But if that is true of contemporary Christian ethics, it certainly wasn't the case in the first three centuries of the church.

27. Augustine, "Patience," 4, 5.
28. Casey, *Balaam's Donkey*, 315.
29. Hauerwas and Pinches, "Practicing Patience," 167, 175.

2

Patience

A Way of Life—The Character Trait on Which the Christian Mission and the Church Depend

ALAN KREIDER HAS PROVIDED us with a narrative of early Christianity that establishes the important role the virtue of patience plays when it comes to the mission of the church. In the face of widespread persecution and even a pandemic, the church of the first three centuries grew because it demonstrated patience.[1]

Early Christians realized that defending their faith with vengeance and bloodshed would only pollute what they were trying to promote. They refused to compel worship, manipulate outcomes, or force compliance; they would even talk with and listen to their critics in a patient approach to mission: "When Christians offered the world not just theological statements but embodied virtue, when they backed up their assertions 'not only in words but also in examples drawn from reality,' they attracted people who felt an irresistible pull to join them."[2]

Kreider is borrowing the concept of "embodied virtue" from the sociologist Pierre Bourdieu. Bourdieu uses the word *habitus*

---

1. Kreider, *Patient Ferment*.
2. Kreider, *Patient Ferment*, 55.

to express this concept, and in our context it refers to a way of life that is rooted in the biblical narrative and especially in the teachings of Jesus that, over time and with practice, becomes embodied and habitual—second nature. For the early church patience was a predisposition that exhibited itself in reflexive behavior learned through repeated bodily action. Particularly by means of catechesis and worship, those who had been nurtured in a habitus inconsistent with the way of Jesus would learn to embody virtues such as patience that would be expressed even in everyday tasks. As Kreider puts it, "This is knowledge that is not taught but inhaled. . . . It is habitus that constitutes our profoundest sense of identity; that forms our deepest convictions, allegiances, and repulsions; and that shapes our response to ultimate questions—what we will live for, die for, and kill (or not kill) for."[3]

This was much more than a laid back approach to life. In a time of persecution *and* plague (ca. 250), Cyprian urged his people to actively live lives marked by the habitus of patience—to trust God, refuse to *control* the outcome, love enemies, live unconventionally. Inexplicable to the pagans who observed it, the Christian witness was embodied as Christians ended up doing good for *all* people, not just their own. Cyprian urged nonviolence as a crucial component of the rehabituated lifestyle of patience: not returning violence for violence, accepting oppression, overcoming anger, refusing to curse or slander, accepting martyrdom, and forgiving others.[4]

Tertullian sees such patience connected with the Beatitudes in Jesus' Sermon on the Mount. Only the patient can be humble ("poor in spirit"). Weepers and mourners who bear unhappiness are those who have patience. The impatient cannot be gentle. Tertullian insists that even a fool can see that the impatient have no affinity with peace as peacemakers. And rejoicing as often as we are cursed and persecuted is only for the patient.[5]

Going a bit further into the sermon, citing Jesus' admonition to turn the other cheek and go the extra mile, Justin Martyr

3. Kreider, *Patient Ferment*, 39–41, 165–66.

4. Kreider, *Patient Ferment*, 66–69, 277.

5. Tertullian, "Patience," 11.

defended the way of Christians who are patient when injured, ready to serve all, and free from anger. Instead of imitating wicked people, Jesus had exhorted the church "to lead all people, by patience and gentleness, from shame and the love of evil." And this had been demonstrated in the case of those converts who had "changed their violent and tyrannical disposition."[6]

For Tertullian, Jesus' parables illustrated how such patience promoted the church's mission. A shepherd finds one straying sheep: "for Impatience would easily despise *one* lamb; but patience takes on the hard work of the quest, and the patient burden-bearer carries home on his shoulders the forsaken sinner." Witness the prodigal father who receives his son over against the angry brother's impatience: "Repentance perishes not, because it finds Patience [to welcome it]."[7]

But the habitus of patience is cultivated not only for the purpose of evangelism; it is also *within* the Christian community that patience must become a way of life. Within the friendships of the monastic community, John Cassian insists that patience is to be promoted not by mere lip service, but laid up in the deepest recesses of the soul. Cassian highlights the patience with which Christian brothers and sisters resist the urge to avenge themselves:

> Patience must be observed not by words but by the inner tranquility of the heart, which commands that we must hold to it when something adverse occurs in such a way that we not only keep ourselves far from wrathful disturbance but also, by submitting to their mistreatment, urge those who have been aroused by their wickedness to return to calm now that they are sated with their blow. Thus we shall conquer their rage with our mildness, and thus we shall also fulfill the apostolic words: "Do not be overcome by evil, but overcome evil with good."[8]

A "genuine humility of heart . . . will glow with the clearest indications of patience" when one disregards accusations and

---

6. Quoted in Sider, ed., *Early Church*, 24.

7. Tertullian, "Patience," 12.

8. Cassian, *Conferences*, 16.22.

Waiting for God, Justice, and Rush-Hour Traffic

endures insults "with a gentle and placid spirit."[9] Such patience is admirable when it is exercised in the context of adversity. In fact, Cassian insists that true patience is strengthened and sharpened when we experience suffering and endurance (from which, he reminds us, patience takes its name). If you are angry, don't blame it on the inflicted abuse; blame it on a "hidden weakness," or, as a Bourdieu disciple might say, on the absence of a Christian habitus.[10]

Again, it is Cyprian who resonates with this concept of habitus so forcefully—with the notion that patience is not to be episodic or momentary, but a way of life in *every* aspect of life for the one who abides in Christ:

> The virtue of patience is displayed in many ways, and its productivity and bigheartedness proceed from a source of one name, yet it spreads out by overflowing streams through many ways of glory. . . . It is patience which both commends us to God and links us to God. It is also patience which softens anger, which bridles the tongue, governs the mind, guards peace, rules discipline, breaks the force of lust, represses the violence of pride, extinguishes the fire of hatred, checks the power of the rich, soothes the want of the poor, protects a blessed integrity in virgins, a careful purity in widows, in those who are united and married [to] a single affection. It makes people humble in prosperity, brave in adversity, gentle towards wrongs and ridicule. It teaches us to pardon quickly those who wrong us; and if you do wrong, to plead long and earnestly for pardon. It resists temptations, suffers persecutions, makes passions and martyrdoms pure. It is patience which firmly fortifies the foundations of our faith. It is this which lifts up on high the increase of our hope. It is this which directs our doing, that we may stick to the way of Christ while we walk by His patience. It is this that makes it possible for us to persevere as children of God, which we imitate our Father's patience.[11]

9. Cassian, *Conferences*, 16.11.
10. Cassian, *Conferences*, 18.13
11. Cyprian, "Patience," 20.

14

Who knew this virtue accomplishes so much!

Casey amplifies the concept of abiding that is a cousin of patience. The Johannine Gospel and epistles use the Greek word for abide (*menein*) about sixty-five times, telling us that believers follow Christ into the life of God and abide there. And this has a behavioral component. "We are to commit ourselves to the struggle of perseverance, knowing that it is not enough to begin a journey; we have to follow it to the end." In other words, it is a way of life that enjoys the happy experiences of springtime, but also weathers the "inevitable spells of dormancy" in bleak winters, so that abiding takes the form of sheer dogged patience, during which "the land must quietly lie fallow until the time for plowing and sowing arrives." And this will require the proactive effort of remembering what we have learned from the biblical narrative and the words of Jesus.[12]

The early church would concur. But, sadly, perhaps not the contemporary church. Archbishop Rowan Williams insists the church today is not exempt from the spirit of the age in which we live—"an age dramatically impatient and intolerant of many sorts of learning." He writes of certain Anglican divines in the past who were "apologists for a theologically informed and spiritually sustained patience":

> They do not expect human words to solve their problems rapidly, they do not expect the Bible to yield up its treasures overnight, they do not look for the triumphant march of an ecclesiastical institution. They know that as Christians they live among immensities of meaning, live in the wake of a divine action which defies summary explanation. They take for granted that the believer is always learning, moving in and out of speech and silence in a continuous wonder and a continuous turning inside-out of mind and feeling.[13]

Indeed, this does not sound like many Christian churches today that want quick conversions verified, not by a way of life, but by

12. Casey, *Balaam's Donkey*, 5–6.
13. Williams, *Anglican Identities*, 7–8.

a boiler plate sinner's prayer. Unlike the early church's habitus of patience, many contemporary Christians seek revenge on those who would upset their sensibilities with their words, actions, or laws. Many try to impose their will on those with whom they disagree.

Evidence of this was on both sides of the political spectrum during the months of COVID restrictions. Those who disagreed with masking and vaccination requirements could not tolerate churches that required them. I witnessed church members who left the fellowship as a result. On the other hand, those who failed to understand why there might be resistance to such requirements were sometimes intolerant of those who did not comply. Patience and tolerance were lacking in a situation that was *temporary*, and, as a result, relationships with those with whom one would be in an *eternal* fellowship were ruptured such that the church's witness became subservient to ideological commitments.

And so, before we continue, we should join Tertullian in his prayer of confession that he offered as he composed his treatise on patience with full self-awareness:

> I fully confess unto the Lord God that it has been rash enough, if not even imprudent, in me to have dared [talk about] Patience, for I am unfit to practice it, being a man of no goodness. . . . So I, most miserable, always sick with the passion of *im*patience, must necessarily and constantly ask and plead for that health of patience which I do not possess; while I recall . . . *the truth*, that the good health of faith, and the soundness of the Lord's discipline, accrue not easily to any unless patience sit by his side.[14]

As he reminds us, nothing can be done that is pleasing to the Lord apart from patience.

---

14. Tertullian, "Patience," 1.

3

The Patient God

GOD IS NOT IN a hurry. And the most visible sign of that is the incarnation. So claimed the early church father Tertullian.

Ever since first reading Tertullian's treatise on patience, my thoughts during Midnight Mass on Christmas Eve go back to his amazing claim that God is so patient that God waited in the womb of Mary for nine months: "God suffers Himself to be conceived in a mother's womb, and awaits the time for birth; and, when born, bears the delay of growing up; and, when grown up, is not eager to be recognized."[1] For nine months in a womb or for three days in a tomb, God goes about work on our behalf. In fact, God is the first example of patience in Tertullian's treatise because, unlike most of us, God is so patient with the unjust and ungrateful "that by His own patience He disparages Himself," which, according to Tertullian, is the reason many of his contemporaries did not believe in the Lord.[2] Of course, the same could be said of many of *our* contemporaries who ask where God is when evil is rampant. (We will have more to say about that in a later chapter when we consider how to respond to God's silence.)

1. Tertullian, "Patience," 3.
2. Tertullian, "Patience," 2.

But for Tertullian and for us a seemingly self-disparaging God is the only God we are going to get, because patience is God's nature. Cyprian concurred: "In God patience has its beginning, and from Him as its source it takes its splendor and dignity. The origin and greatness of patience proceeds from God its Author."[3] Karl Barth is even more emphatic: "It is His being. Everything that God is, is implied and included in the statement that He is patient."[4]

Just as we were warned against counterfeit patience by John Cassian, so Barth assures us that God's patience is not only distinguished from all forms of impatience, "but no less from all the weak, non-divine and therefore false patience which derives from indifference or weakness or shortsightedness."[5] For this reason Barth insists that "long-suffering" is a bad translation for the Greek word *makrothymia* if it suggests "hesitation, weakness, indulgence, a stretching of the divine will." Instead, "the term implies that God's will is great and strong and relentless and victorious," as God's waiting gives human creatures "every freedom and opportunity."[6] This is *not* "an indifferent self-withdrawal of God" if we understand God's patience correctly. It is an "undeniable risk" that God took in creating the other, but a risk in which God was "more than a match."[7]

God purposefully concedes time and space to creatures. God *could* be gracious and merciful in such a way that it would consume the creature. Instead, God allows an other the time and space for its own development as a reality alongside God, "fulfilling His will towards this other in such a way that He does not suspend and destroy it as this other but accompanies and sustains it and allows it to develop in freedom."[8] God takes up the cause of the creature, even sacrificing God's only Son for it. God's grace *will* uphold and

3. Quoted in Hauerwas and Pinches, "Practicing Patience," 172. See Exod 34:6, Ps 145:8.

4. Barth, *CD* II/1:408.

5. Barth, *CD* II/1:423.

6. Barth, *CD* II/1:410.

7. Barth, *CD* III/1:109.

8. Barth, *CD* III/1:409–10.

eventually control this other, not by destroying the other, but by judging it, radically transforming it, and renewing it.[9]

So, for Barth, "God's forbearance is only a specific form of His always powerful doing and being. God is therefore no less effective in His patience than in His grace and mercy, than in His holy and just wrath which includes His grace and mercy." God's self-restraint is "the powerful act of God" without which God would be *less* divine—in fact, *not God at all*.[10]

We can see this expressed in Isaiah 55, where the prophet implores the readers to seek the Lord and forsake their ways and unrighteous thoughts, because Yahweh's thoughts are not our thoughts and Yahweh's ways are not our ways. People are mistaken who think that in this passage Yahweh's thoughts are not our thoughts means that God is telling us that the divine is beyond rational knowledge, as true as that might be. That is not the context of this statement. The point Isaiah is making is that God has mercy on us and freely pardons us *because* God's thoughts and ways are not ours whose patience wears thin and who seek revenge instead of pardon. God has time, and time to wait for us. Our impatient thoughts and ways are not godlike.

God does not punish us immediately. For a time God passes over past sins (Rom 3:25). But because of that, the interval between our misdeeds and God's final judgment is one reason there is so much suffering. As my former professor Diogenes Allen reminds us, this does not mean that God is doing nothing: "God is exercising his mercy. Our redemption means enduring evil, so that we may repent of it." And one aspect of this repentance is agreement with God's way of doing things. When we pray, "Thy will be done," we are also agreeing with God's decision to be merciful to all. Those who acknowledge the patience entailed in God's mercy must also repent of their impatience with the resultant "long, groaning, struggle-filled history of human life."[11]

9. Barth, *CD* III/1:411.

10. Barth, *CD* III/1:410. Note the relationship between God's patience and God's action, a topic we will highlight later as the creative activity of patience.

11. Allen, *Steps Along the Way*, 100–101.

God forbears our sin (Rom 2:4, 3:25; 2 Pet 3:9)—not over-looking our sin, but patiently waiting us out in order to lead us to repent and change our ways. As Stanley Hauerwas and Samuel Wells put it when they defined the word "world" in terms of the long-suffering of God, "The world is all that in God's creation have taken the opportunity of God's patience not yet to believe in him."[12]

So, God's patience is not abandonment of divine providential oversight. In the story of Cain, God does not will the death that Cain deserves; instead, God binds God's self to a sinful human in a kind of treaty. In the story of Noah, after forty days of rain, God gives himself space to speak and act further with God's creatures. In the story of Jonah, an impatient God would be a petty, human, weak, and false deity—a lesson Jonah has to learn the hard way. Initially, in God's answer to Moses' intercession for an impatient people who could not wait for Moses to come down from the mountain, God's "nose is hot" wishing to destroy the nation and start over; but God becomes "long of nose" (i.e., shows no anger) in response to Moses' prayer, providing a new insight into God's character (Exod 34:6).[13] In all of these cases, the real aim and in-tention when God exercises patience is to uphold all things by the power of God's Word—the powerful Word of the Son (Heb 1:3).[14]

Barth brings all of this home when he emphatically states that "to see and hear and feel and recognize the power of this patience means to believe in Jesus Christ." This is an amazing claim that deserves pondering. God can allow creatures their freedom to go their own way and wait for them because God has already over-taken his creatures in God's Son. God is not giving creatures space and time to continue in their impenitence, but to "appropriate the life that has already been secured for them by the sincere penitence of the Son."[15] Donato Ogliari draws an astounding implication from this when he suggests that God's patience includes suffering

12. Hauerwas and Wells, "Gift of the Church," 21.

13. See Dozeman, "Patience," 353; the phrases about noses are literal trans-lations of the Hebrew.

14. Barth, *CD* II/1:412–16.

15. Barth, *CD* II/1:418–19.

by virtue of God's sovereign and free will (unlike we who suffer by virtue of our creaturely limitations and violence): "In Christ's life, passion and death, we have the mysterious and supreme manifestation of God's patience, his definitive answer to sinful and ungrateful mankind."[16] And this paradigm found in Christ "enlightens and gives sense to human patience and, as a consequence, to our experience of suffering."[17] As we share in God's sufferings (Col 1:24), we participate in God's patience!

So, God's patience is a summons to us to have faith. God knows us in the Person of the One who is our Head and Representative, so "that which he awaits has taken place and is fulfilled, the obedience which He demands from His creature has been rendered." The final outcome that God has predetermined makes our preservation "meaningful and necessary."[18] This is why Christian hope is integral for Christian patience, as we will discuss later.

This perspective is not unlike Barth's notion that the covenant that God made with his creatures in eternity past (such as the *protoevangelium* in Genesis 3:15) demands a stage upon which the covenant is to be played out. So the covenant becomes the internal basis of creation, and the creation becomes the external means of the covenant. In the context of God's patience, Barth puts it this way:

> It [the creature's preservation] is necessary because God has linked His own life with ours, and has sacrificed Himself for us so that as truly as God Himself lives we cannot perish. As we are summoned by the patience of God to the life of faith, we are invited to seize and affirm this *objective divine justification of our existence and with it the justification of the divine patience itself,* for our own part giving God the glory which He has assured Himself by creating and establishing this *ground for His patience.*[19]

So God's patience is intentional to the praise of God's own glory: "God is not the slave of His patience. . . . What moves Him

16. Ogliari, *"Laus Patientiae,"* 7.

17. Ogliari, *"Laus Patientiae,"* 12.

18. Barth, *CD* II/1:419.

19. Barth, *CD* II/1:419, emphasis added.

to exercise patience is His holy and righteous, gracious and merciful meaning, His will to unfold to us this meaning, to lead us to penitence, and therefore to make our own lives meaningful." In other words, "Jesus Christ is the meaning of God's patience."[20] Cyprian would not quite put it as Barth does, but he would concur that the purpose of God's patience is that we who are "involved in the contagion of errors and crimes, may, *even though late*, be converted to God" (appealing to Ezek 18:32, Mal 3:7, Joel 2:13, and Rom 2:4–6).[21] God does not overlook or forget our sin, but forbears it, making possible our deliverance from sin and God's wrath, and our conversion to new life. Perhaps it is better said that God's patient forgiveness means that God remembers our sin in a new way.[22]

And this all leads Cyprian to insist that if God is the author of patience, and if God is our Lord and Father, then we are to imitate God's patience, and in so doing we become like God as living examples of God's mercy toward others (Matt 5:43–48).[23] The parable of the unforgiving servant in Matthew 18:21–35, which comes immediately after Jesus' admonition to Peter that he must forgive an offending brother 490 times (which really means that if you are counting you are not forgiving), makes the connection between divine and human patience in the most dramatic fashion. Our patience is to be modeled after God's. This means, as Michael Casey says, "we may not preempt the action of grace" in others. He quotes Augustine: "Don't despair of those who are now what you used to be." This requires a significant trust in divine providence and acting in God's time.[24]

---

20. Barth, *CD* II/1:432. Ogliari would concur: "It is revelation itself, as it is incarnated in the life of Jesus, that tells us of the Father's total engagement in his Son's mission, including his passion and death. So in Jesus' life, and above all in his passion and death, God's patience finds its fulfillment." Ogliari, *"Laus Patientiae,"* 10.

21. Cyprian, "Patience," 4, emphasis added.

22. Wadell, *Becoming Friends,* 168.

23. Cyprian, "Patience," 3, 5.

24. Casey, *Balaam's Donkey,* 244–45.

Richard Mouw helps us see the implications of the relationship between God's patience and the need for ours in our own social location. He dwells on a wonderful phrase the Mennonites have that describes our present situation as Christians: "'We are 'living in the time of God's patience.' If God is patient, we must be also." He argues that in our political life we must exercise this patience in our democratic system "with a willingness to find less-than-perfect solutions," recognizing—and recalling what was said about habitus—that "it does take some effort to cultivate that kind of patience." And since we live in a time before the judgment day arrives, "when righteousness and unrighteousness exist side by side, believers must establish their patterns of living with this fact in mind."[25]

Though it is long, Tertullian's personification of God's patience is an appropriate conclusion to reflect on the theological truth we have unpacked.

> God is a sufficiently sufficient Treasurer of patience. If you deposit in his care a wrong done to you, God is an Avenger; if a loss, God is a Restorer; if pain, God is a Healer; if death, God is a Reviver. What honor is granted to Patience, to have God as her Debtor! And not without reason: for she keeps all God's decrees; she has to do with all God's mandates. She fortifies faith; is the pilot of peace; assists charity; establishes humility; waits long for repentance; sets her seal on confession; rules the flesh; preserves the spirit; bridles the tongue; restrains the hand; tramples temptations under foot; drives away scandals; gives crowning grace to martyrdoms; consoles the poor; teaches the rich moderation; does not overstrain the weak; does not exhaust the strong; is the delight of the believer; invites the Gentile; commends the servant to the master, and his master to God; adorns the woman; makes the man approved; is loved in childhood, praised in youth, looked up to in age; is beautiful in either sex, in every time of life. . . . Her countenance is tranquil and peaceful; her brow serene, contracted by no wrinkles of sadness or of anger; her eyebrows evenly relaxed in gladsome wise, with eyes downcast in humility,

25. Mouw, *Abraham Kuyper*, 108, 111.

not in unhappiness; her mouth sealed with the honorable mark of silence; her hue such as theirs who are without care and without guilt; the motion of her head frequent against the devil, and her laugh threatening; her clothing, moreover, about her breast white and well fitted to her person, as being neither inflated nor disturbed. For Patience sits on the throne of that calmest and gentlest Spirit, who is not found in the roll of the whirlwind, nor in the leaden hue of the cloud, but is of the soft serenity, open and simple. . . . For where God is, there too is God's foster-child, namely Patience. When God's Spirit descends, then Patience accompanies God indivisibly. If we do not admit her together with the Spirit, will God always abide with us? No, I do not know whether God would remain any longer. Without God's companion and handmaid, of necessity God must be limited in every place and at every time. Whatever blow God's enemy may inflict, God will be unable to endure alone, being without the instrumental means of enduring.[26]

---

26. Tertullian, "Patience," 15.

4

Cruciform Patience

THE *DEFINITIVE* REVELATION OF God's patience is Jesus Christ. Like Father, like Son. As Cyprian put it, Christ "maintained the patience of His Father in the constancy of His endurance. . . . all His actions, even from His very advent, are characterized by patience as their partner."[1] He is the perfect union of love, patience, and suffering. "Jesus Christ is the trustee of divine patience. By his incarnation, passion and death, undergone for our justification, he confirms the infinite extent of God's patience."[2]

In the event of the crucifixion, Diogenes Allen captured well how Christ's sacrifice expressed the patience of the Father who allows "creatures who are living unfaithfully to use their power to resist the good that God would bestow." The divine response endures creaturely resistance. But that same divine response—that endurance[3] turns our resistance into a divine sacrifice. Working from the Latin *sacer* and *facere*—"to make holy"—Allen argues that the brutal execution of the patient God is made holy as God

1. Cyprian, "Patience," 6.

2. Ogliari, *"Laus Patientiae,"* 20.

3. The New Testament Greek word translated "endure" or "forbear" is *anechometha*.

25

takes our very rejection and turns it into a revelation of his love—of his willingness to put up with our stone cold hearts and evil. "His response to all that we are and have done is not rejection, but painful endurance. Not only does he let us see the effects of all that we are and have done by letting it destroy his body, but he also shows us that all that we are and have done does not defeat him. His love cannot be turned away."[4]

But can *we* turn away from God's love?

Cyprian believes divine patient sacrificial love is *compelling*. Christ experienced the opposite of what he had been before the incarnation. As incarnate he experienced our flesh, our mortality, being baptized by John, fasting, washing the disciples' feet. He persuaded the unbelieving, soothed the ungrateful, and gently answered his detractors. "He could bear Judas even to the last with a long patience—could take meat with His enemy—could know the household foe, and not openly point him out, nor refuse the kiss of the traitor. . . . Even to the end, all things are borne perseveringly and constantly, in order that in Christ a full and perfect patience may be accomplished."[5]

Cyprian concludes with a profound statement about the extent of Jesus' patience and its intended effect: "And after all these things, He still receives His murderers, if they will be converted and come to Him; and with a saving patience, He who is kindly and benevolent to press on, closes His Church to none. . . . Even he is made alive by Christ's blood who has shed Christ's blood. Such is and so great is the patience of Christ; and had it not been such and so great, the Church would never have possessed Paul as an apostle."[6]

Though such divine patience may have the desired result of a conversion like Paul's, Tertullian was right to admit that this patience, which no human can achieve, is also "a cause for rejection of the faith."[7] Presumably that has something to do with those who

4. Allen, *Steps Along the Way*, 40–41.
5. Cyprian, "Patience," 6, 7.
6. Cyprian, "Patience," 8.
7. Tertullian, "Patience," 3.

mistakenly assume that God simply does not care about injustice. It may be why Cyprian assures those who have been treated unjustly that the day will come when divine justice *will* respond so that we are admonished to wait for that day:

> Let us wait for Him. . . . Let him who hurries, and is too impatient for his revenge, consider that even He Himself is not yet avenged who is the Avenger. . . . How great is the Lord Jesus, and how great is His patience, that He who is adored in heaven is not yet avenged on earth! Let us, beloved brethren, consider His patience in our persecutions and sufferings, . . . let us not hasten, servants as we are, to be defended before our Lord with irreligious and immodest eagerness.[8]

So, in the meantime we wait with a cruciform patience, for, as Barth puts it so well, "If we suffer with Him in this hope, and we believe according to God's Word that we have to suffer with Jesus Christ in this hope, we can and may and must suffer in patience: answering His patience with our patience; giving the right answer to the waiting of His wrath with our waiting for redemption."[9] Christ has not eliminated suffering. Christ has redeemed it by God's participation in Jesus' cross that conquered suffering and death.[10]

To be clear, waiting with a cruciform patience as Christ modeled for us in his suffering is not weakness. It was in the context of self-sacrifice as power that Dorothy Day remarked, "Patience, patience—which means suffering."[11]

This cruciform patience was emphasized a couple centuries after Cyprian in the monastic tradition begun by Benedict. He concludes the Prologue to his Rule with this aspiration: "Never swerving from his [God's] instructions, then, but faithfully observing his teaching in the monastery until death, we shall through patience share in the sufferings of Christ that we may deserve

---

8. Cyprian, "Patience," 23.

9. Barth, *CD* II/1:422.

10. Ogliari, "*Laus Patientiae*," 12.

11. Ellsberg, ed., *Duty of Delight*, quoted in Rutledge, *Crucifixion*, 275.

also to share in his kingdom."[12] Benedict later (7.35) describes the monk who, in "difficult, unfavorable, or even unjust conditions," "quietly embraces suffering." Thus, patience is a fundamental virtue for Benedict and the Christian monastic tradition, connecting it to Christ's passion[13] rather than to Stoic determinism. As the Benedictine scholar Terrence Kardong put it, "For a Christian, of course, the suffering of Christ is the root of all virtue."[14] Hugh Feiss, another Benedictine scholar, expands upon this connection: "Christian efforts to understand suffering inevitably lead to the paschal mystery, the dying and rising of Christ, the seed that must die if it is to bear fruit. Hence suffering can coexist with joy, not because suffering is either unreal or invariably mild, but because it is a path to life."[15]

Kardong insists that the term "patiently" (Latin, *patienter*) is a key element of monastic formation, is never a throwaway word in Benedict's Rule, and is sometimes explicitly connected with the necessity of carrying the cross of Christ: "Etymologically, *patior* (to bear) is an appropriate counterpart to the image of a burden (*pondus oneris*)," which is referred to later in the Rule (68.2) when a monk is asked by the abbot to perform a task that the monk thinks he is unable to accomplish.[16] But the point that needs highlighting is that concepts related to patience, such as *sharing* Christ's passion, *embracing* suffering, and *bearing* a burden, imply that patience is not the virtue of a helpless victim, but a virtue that requires *active* participation. We will explore this aspect of patience in the next chapter.

So, if our patience is modeled after the God revealed in the crucified Christ (Heb 12:2–3), it should be displayed even toward *our* enemies (1 Cor 4:12–13). This can only happen if the heart is widened or enlarged so as to receive, diffuse, and do away with anger.

12. Fry, ed., *RB1980*, Prologue, 50.

13. Note that the word *passion* is a derivative of *pati* in Latin, meaning "suffer," making the link between suffering and patience etymological as well.

14. Kardong, *Benedict's Rule*, 148.

15. Feiss, *Monastic Wisdom*, 133.

16. Kardong, *Benedict's Rule*, 569.

It is similar to widening the diameter of a pipe to relieve the water pressure that flows through it. It is captured in the Greek word *makrothymia*, a word that refers to a prolonged restraint of *thymos*—anger or agitation. (Patience is the countervailing virtue to anger.) And though it is not the word that Paul uses in 2 Corinthians 6:11–13, there is something of the same connotation when the apostle writes, "Our heart is wide open to you. There is no restriction in our affections, only in yours. In return . . . open wide your hearts also." Our hearts might be widened by memories of God's forgiveness of and patience with us, or by visions of future reconciliation.

Apparently such widening is something the unforgiving servant in Jesus' parable was incapable of doing, for which he was reprimanded (Matt 18:26, 29). It is important to note that this parable amplifies what Jesus instructs about church discipline in cases where one has caused offense (18:15–20). The process of resolving the conflict between the offender and offended requires three steps—three chances—before the person is finally dismissed from the fellowship.[17] A widened heart diffuses the anger that constricts one who has been offended so that time is patiently given to consider what is necessary for reconciliation to take place—it if ever does.

In a previous book (*Dangerous Passions, Deadly Sins*[18]), I shared my wife's experience while waiting in line at the grocery store to pay for her groceries. An older man in front of her yelled to a female employee at the next counter whom he thought should be bagging his groceries: "Hey, Stubby, get over here and start doing your job." My wife was stunned. The words were so startling that she was not sure she had assessed the situation correctly, so she asked (with a tinge of sarcasm, since she thought she probably *had* understood correctly), "Were you joking with her or were you talking to another human being that way?" He told her this was none of her business. She replied that it was not right to talk to someone that way. His response did not match his chronological age: he rattled off a list of insults you might hear on an elementary

17. See Hoezee's discussion of this passage in *Riddle of Grace*, 139–47.
18. See pp. 93–94.

school playground, such as, "I'd hate to be your husband and wake up to see your face every morning." (It is clear that he not only lacked emotional maturity, but he also had poor aesthetic judgment.) My wife answered these insults by calmly retorting "I feel sorry for you" and "That's very sad."

My wife's attempt to first understand the intention of the man's comment in the checkout line was an effort to widen her heart with patience and reframe the event. Perhaps she could have paused longer to ask herself if there were other circumstances in this man's life that helped to explain his attitude toward the bagger. But at least her patient pause and attempt to reappraise the situation had the effect of reducing her subsequent verbal aggression.

Of course, such a widened heart has always been the operating procedure of the God who has self-disclosed in the crucified Christ, even as early in the biblical Story as Exodus 34:6–7: "The Lord passed before [Moses], and proclaimed, 'The Lord, the Lord, a God merciful and gracious, slow to anger, and abounding in steadfast love and faithfulness, keeping steadfast love for *the thousandth generation*, forgiving iniquity and transgression and sin, yet by no means clearing the guilty, but visiting the iniquity of the parents upon the children and the children's children, to *the third and the fourth generation*.'"

Many times, in our hurry to point out God's judgment, the latter part of this passage is cited, while the former part, referring to "the thousandth," is neglected. God's steadfast love extends to many more generations than God's judgment. But this slow-to-anger and relenting-from-punishing God is exactly what upset Jonah centuries after Moses (Jonah 4:2).

In the biblical story, Jonah was afflicted with the disease of Ninevitis—a disease not found in the manuals of the AMA or the APA, but a common sickness that manifests itself in the desire to limit the reach of God's love. Jonah had admirable characteristics: he believed in *Yahweh*, believed God had a plan for his life, was capable of an heroic act to save the lives of innocent sailors, and even loved humanity—in general. The problem is that God was not interested in generalities. God got specific: Jonah must love

Nineveh. That wasn't easy once we realize that it was a symbol of overwhelming ruthless power comparable to modern-day ISIS (see Nah 3:1, 19). God wants to offer them the possibility of divine amnesty in exchange for repentance. God has already been slow to anger with Jonah, patiently waiting for his servant to embrace the call of scandalous, inclusive mercy—the divine quality that God wants to cultivate in this judgement-obsessed prophet.

But then "Ninevitis" strikes. There *is* human evil, and God *is* a God of justice and wrath who will bring his kingdom agenda to earth as it is in heaven. But, like Jonah, we are impatient with God's wrathful justice (which God *will* bestow on Nineveh later). We want it *now*, and, like Jonah, we who are God's people are sometimes tempted to view God's reluctant wrath as indecisiveness or inconsistency to the point that we will even taunt God as Jonah did in 4:3: "Please take my life from me, O Lord, for it is better for me to die than to live." In other words, "If you aren't going to give these people what's coming to them, then I'm out of here. Just kill me. I dare you! Destroy me or destroy Nineveh."

Jonah needs a cure for Ninevitis. *We* need a cure for Ninevitis. What Jonah and we need to cultivate is the habitus of "long-suffering" that we have been unpacking. It is the patience that desires what God desires—to see everyone come to repentance. This is not indifference. It is the merciful patience spoken of in 2 Peter 3:9–10: "The Lord is not slow in keeping his promise, as some understand slowness. Instead, he is patient with you, not wanting anyone to perish, but everyone to come to repentance. But the day of the Lord will come like a thief." And note that the text says "you," not "them." We are to remember the times that *we* have been the recipient of God's patient grace as we impatiently anticipate and pray for God's justice. This is a lesson Jonah will learn under the shade of a divinely planted tree that Jonah doesn't deserve.

Self-diagnosis requires that we ask ourselves if we have been infected with Ninevitis. It *is* contagious. We can catch it from the media—even some Christian media. The self-diagnosis begins with a question: Who is my "Nineveh"? And then the cure begins with another question: When in the past have I experienced God's mercy in giving *me* a second chance—mercy that I can share with my "Nineveh"?

After all, at one time or another all of us have probably been someone else's Nineveh. Twentieth-century Cistercian monk Thomas Merton thought as much when he wrote these words:

> Do not be too quick to assume your enemy is a savage just because he is *your* enemy. Perhaps he is your enemy because he thinks you are a savage. Do not be too quick to assume that your enemy is an enemy of God just because is *your* enemy. Perhaps he is your enemy precisely because he can find nothing in you that gives glory to God. Perhaps he fears you because he can find nothing in you of God's love and God's kindness and God's patience and mercy and understanding of the weaknesses of men.[19]

Long after Jonah this all hit home again when Jesus came on the scene. Before Jesus would demonstrate divine patience in his trial and death, Jesus illustrated such patience in his story of Lazarus and Dives. In his discussion of the parable, New Testament scholar Kenneth Bailey helps us with his examination of New Testament Greek words for "patience."[20]

Bailey begins by pointing out that Paul's list of the characteristics of love begins with one form of patience (*makrothymia*) and ends with a second form of patience (*hypomone*). The first is composed of *makran* (far away) and *thymos* (anger). So, as was mentioned above, it has to do with "putting far away one's anger"—a prolonged restraint of anger, even toward one's enemies. Bailey argues that this is exemplified by the patience of David when he stood over the sleeping body of Saul (1 Sam 26:6–25)—the patience of one who is powerful enough to exact vengeance on his enemy, but instead chooses to exercise patience and refrain from the violent act. As Bailey says, "David exhibited *makrothymia* and stayed his hand."

The second form of patience combines *hypo* (under) with *mone* (having to do with endurance or "long-suffering"). Bailey

19. Merton, *New Seeds of Contemplation*, 177.
20. Bailey, *Jesus Through Middle Eastern Eyes*, 389–903 for what follows.

suggests that this virtue's primary biblical example is Mary, who chose to remain silently at the foot of the cross. And he finds in Jesus' parable of Lazarus and Dives that the former exhibits both forms of patience—*makrothymia* and *hypomone*, especially since one expects Lazarus to explode in a rage of anger. Instead, "In his earthly life he had no complaints, he was long-suffering and full of *hypomone*. When, in a position of power, at the side of Abraham, he demonstrates *makrothymia*, he puts his anger far away." Bailey concludes: "Lazarus created meaning by what he chose to do. He was quiet in his days of powerless suffering, and remained silent in his days of power as he listened to his former tormenter demand services from him."

Should Lazarus have protested? Hugh Feiss argues that we accept some injustices because they are unavoidable. We might protest others but should not, because the good achieved by protest would not outweigh the damage caused by protest. And then there *are* times when we are obliged to protest. Feiss insists that other than cases requiring obligatory protest,

> one should bear persecution for justice's sake. Such patience is a gift, rooted in the faith that God is in charge of the universe, and that God's Providence can and will bring good out of bad. . . . Suffering entered into willingly leads us to the will of God, which may not be what we wanted or hoped for. Accepting annoyances and suffering as special gifts of God who loves us to perfection may take us out of ourselves and show us, in other people, the face of Christ turned toward us.[21]

To illustrate Feiss's point, Cyprian would point us to Christ before Pilate. To the wonder of Pilate, Jesus kept a patient silence. What Feiss may imply by God's providence is made explicit by Cyprian, for endurance in the face of injustice that puts vengeful anger far away (*makrothymia*) requires trust that God is faithfully just. As we have already heard from Cyprian in this matter, we revisit it in its context. In the case of Jesus before Pilate, "although He was silent in His passion, yet by and by He will not be silent in His

---

21. Feiss, *Monastic Wisdom*, 133–34.

vengeance. . . . For although He came first shrouded in humility, yet He shall come manifest in power. . . . Let us wait for Him. . . . Let him who hurries, and is too impatient for his revenge, consider that even He Himself is not yet avenged who is the Avenger. . . . How great is the Lord Jesus, and how great is His patience, that He who is adored in heaven is not yet avenged on earth!"[22]

Cyprian could just as well have called our attention to the fact that Jesus abstained from exposing his betrayer as he washed his feet, refused to avenge his betrayer, complied with his arrest, and even showed compassion for the suffering of Malchus whose ear Peter had severed.

Tertullian suggested a less theological rationale for enduring injustice with patience. He thought wickedness, violence, blows inflicted, and slander might be "wearied out" by patience, which he identified as "the *utility* and *pleasure* of patience." It is pleasurable because the patient one denies the inflictor the joy he would derive from the pain suffered, so the one who ends up being pained is the one who lost his enjoyment at seeing the victim patiently endure. The patient one is revenged by the inflictor's pain.[23]

There are portrayals of this in novels and movies. There is a scene in the movie *Unbroken* when the prisoner Louis "Louie" Zamperini is punished by the Japanese camp commander, ordered to hold a large wooden beam over his head, to be shot if he dropped it. He defiantly holds it up, enraging the commander as Louie stares at him. The commander is so incensed by Louie's endurance that he beats him. Nonetheless, the inflictor of pain is denied the joy he expected if Louie had not endured.

What Tertullian does not seem to take into account, however, is that the perpetrator who treats another unjustly must have some degree of a moral conscience for this to work. This must have been the case in 1963 when Martin Luther King Jr. and other black leaders organized peaceful demonstrations in Birmingham, Alabama. Against peaceful protestors, city commissioner of public safety, Eugene "Bull" Connor, responded with fire hoses and attack dogs,

22. Cyprian, "Patience," 23.
23. Tertullian, "Patience," 8.

but the public was wearied out by televised images of Connor's violence against the patient nonviolent behavior. As a result, the American opinion that civil rights was the most urgent issue in the US went from 4 percent of the population before the incident to 52 percent after it. And the next year Congress passed the Civil Rights Act.[24] "Bull" Connor's "pleasure" was diminished, but it was the moral conscience of the American populace, not "Bull" Connor's, that made it possible.

If we remove extreme cases that require heroics—the kind that *is* often portrayed in novels and movies but might also be the "extra mile" Jesus demanded of the disciple in the Sermon on the Mount—we are left with everyday situations that require a more ordinary exercise of cruciform patience. Michael Casey puts it this way: "Many are the heroes of major battles who fall by ambush in unguarded moments." So he assures us that patience is not "mindless endurance," but "the willingness to relive in one's own situation that form of life chosen by Jesus for himself. What matters most is our practical acceptance of the way of Christ," which Casey says will animate us with boundless compassion for the weaknesses and sufferings of fellow humans.[25] This requires an internal equilibrium that quietly endures unjust slightings, insults, snubs, minor injuries, and the like—even at the hand of enemies, and not simply as a victim, but as one who actively participates in the suffering. It is in these situations that we are to exercise cruciform patience, which might also be a way of cultivating the "extra mile" type *makrothymia* that is characteristic of *hypomone*.

As Paul wrote to the Corinthians of his ministry, "When reviled, we bless; when persecuted, we endure; when slandered, we speak kindly. We have become like the rubbish of the world, the dregs of all things, to this very day" (1 Cor 4:12–13). Or consider the central theme in the sermon to the Hebrews—that of perseverance (*hypomone*) in contrast to falling away (*hypostole*) in the face of suffering, exposure to insult and persecution, and confiscation of personal property (Heb 10:32–39); we endure such suffering

24. Berger, *US Constitution*, 199–200.
25. Casey, *Living in the* Truth, 111–12.

following the example of the crucified Christ (12:1–3). And even more radical is the imperative to submit to earthly obligations, such as obedience to the state and indentured servility, because Christ left us the example of refusing to return abuse for abuse or threatening retaliation when suffering, serving us by his death and entrusting himself to divine justice (1 Pet 2:13–25).

If we are honest we must admit that such imperatives do not sit well with us. When I informed him of this book project, a friend of mine forewarned me that I would get pushback for even rehearsing these imperatives in light of racial and gender violence in our history. That is understandable.[26]

Given what seem to be divine constraints on defiance and resistance, is it possible to misconstrue what Scripture demands and Jesus exemplifies? Or is there a God-ordained time and place for fighting against injustice without delay, especially on behalf of those who have been marginalized or beaten down? The answer to both questions has to be a resounding "yes." Yet, how can this be, given all that has been said about the cruciform nature of Christian patience? More will be said on this in chapter 5, but on the way to answering, it is worthwhile to be instructed with the contemporary case of one who *was* on the margins practicing cruciform patience.

For sometimes *children* can teach us as they exhibit divine long-suffering amidst violence. When my oldest granddaughter, Clara, was four and visiting us, I pulled out our picture book entitled *The Story of Ruby Bridges*, by Robert Coles. (A book written by Bridges herself was recently banned in a Florida school district.) This is the story of that little first grader whom a judge ordered to go to a white elementary school in New Orleans in 1960 because the state refused to comply with desegregation laws. Ruby and her family prayed long and hard for her to be strong and have courage. Every day she was escorted by federal marshals through angry crowds with signs that said they didn't want black kids in a white school, calling her names and shouting that they wanted to hurt her. And every day Ruby attended school *alone*; the rest of the class

26. See Kendi, "*Patience* Is a Dirty Word."

refused to attend if she was present. She got down to the task of learning with calm and confidence. Her teacher, Miss Hurley, was amazed and thought Ruby would eventually give up. One day Miss Hurley saw Ruby walk up to the building and stop in the midst of the crowd. She asked Ruby what she was saying to the people, and Ruby grew irritated. She told Miss Hurley, "I didn't stop and talk with them. I wasn't talking. I was praying. I was praying for them." It turned out that every morning Ruby stopped a few blocks away from the school to say a prayer for the people who hated her. That morning she forgot until she was already in the middle of the angry mob. When school was over that day, she walked a few blocks from the hateful crowd and prayed the prayer she prayed every day before and after school: "Please God, try to forgive these people because even if they say those bad things, they don't know what they're doing. So you could forgive them, just like You did those folks a long time ago when they said terrible things about You."[27]

My granddaughter asked me to read that book three times, and I would have read it a fourth time as she requested if I had had the kind of long-suffering we've been discussing. Jonah could have learned a thing or two from Ruby. We certainly can.

Indeed, the world would be better if we could be Christlike patient disciples, as Michael Casey puts it so well: "If we wish to minimize evil in the world, our best means of accomplishing this is to absorb it within our own lives, like Christ, to bear the sins of the world. Not to react to the petty prickles of social living, but with a quiet mind to embrace the way of Christ, making sure that the suffering inflicted on us is not reprocessed and then passed on to others."[28]

But *is* this quiet "absorption" of patience simply milquetoast acquiescence? Even Jesus' silence before Pilate cannot be characterized as such. How so? Much like nonviolent resistance that characterizes pacifism, to answer that we need to consider the creative activity of patience.

27. Coles, *Ruby Bridges*, 23.
28. Casey, *Balaam's Donkey*, 316.

5

The Creative Activity of Patience

CHRISTIAN PATIENCE IS ACTIVE and creative. An oft-quoted piece of wisdom allegedly from Leo Tolstoy put it this way: "Patience is waiting. Not passively waiting. That is laziness. But to keep going when the going is hard and slow—that is patience. The two most powerful warriors are patience and time."

The patient warrior is not a slave to passions that are counterproductive. In his discussion of the virtue of fortitude citing Thomas Aquinas, Josef Pieper admits that patience has come to mean "an indiscriminate, self-immolating, crabbed, joyless, spineless submission to whatever evil is met with or, worse, deliberately sought out." On the contrary, Pieper insists that the patient person is not one who is sad and confused, but one who maintains "cheerfulness and serenity of mind in spite of injuries that result from the realization of the good," and as such, it does not exclude "energetic, forceful activity."[1] As Joyce Meyers put it, "Patience is not simply the ability to wait. It's how we behave while we're waiting."[2]

Philosopher Robert C. Roberts tells us that patience is not aimlessness, because the "aimless person has become trained not

1. Pieper, *Cardinal Virtues*, 129.
2. Frequently quoted online and ascribed to Joyce Meyers.

to have any concerns, while in the dispositionally patient person certain [sustained] concerns or passions [that characterize the patient person] have become so dominant that the impulses which beset most people no longer exist." And the patient *Christian's* governing passion is the kingdom of God.[3]

Such patience makes it possible for us to maintain commitments for lifetime projects, such as marriage, friendships, eradicating racially based inequality—even when there are reasons to give up (discouragements, difficulties, temptations, and the like). Such dispositionally patient persons have the ability to count the cost of such projects without being *passively* in the grip of a passion; they are persons "who direct their own lives and therefore have sufficient insight into what they are doing and who they are and what their options are to be able to choose intelligently."[4] They actively persevere.

As James illustrates, the farmer patiently waits for the land to yield its crop and for the rains to nourish the earth (5:7–8). Impatiently digging up the seeds to see if they are growing would be ruinous. The kind of patience James refers to allows us to let endurance have its effect in character cultivation (Jas 1:2–4). In the parable of the sower, Jesus implies the same—seed must remain in good soil to yield a hundredfold, bearing fruit "with patient endurance (*hypomone*)" (Luke 8:8, 15).

The *Rule of Benedict* makes it clear that the character development of such dispositionally patient people requires not only *our* patience, but the patience of *God*:

> Having finished his discourse [the Sermon on the Mount], the Lord waits for us to respond by action every day to his holy warnings. Therefore the days of this life are given us as a time of truce for the correction of our faults. The Apostle says, "Don't you know that the patience of God leads you to repentance?" (Rom 2:4). For the Lord in his benevolence says: "I do not wish the death of the sinner, but rather that he change his ways

3. Roberts, *Christian Character*, 65–66.
4. Roberts, *Christian Character*, 83–84, 92.

and live" (Ezek 33:11). So we know what is required of "dwellers in his tent" and the question is whether we will fulfill the duties of an "inhabitant."[5]

As Terrence Kardong comments, the *makrothymia* referred to here in Romans 2:4 also means "allowing another the time to develop or change," since, like God, we must often refrain from impatient anger to give space for character to take shape in others.[6] So patience—human and divine—allows lives to bubble and foam like the yeast I put in warm water while I put together the rest of my corn bread waffle recipe for our Saturday morning breakfast routine. In other words, things are *happening* with patience. Stanley Hauerwas put it this way: "I am often in a hurry and busy, but this is not the same thing as impatience. Patience does not mean 'doing nothing.' Rather, patience is 'sticking to' what you are doing because you believe that it is worthy and worthwhile."[7] It can be that lifetime project.

What "sticking to" refers to is the *hypomone* we discussed in the previous chapter. And like the warm water that is necessary for the yeast, it is by sticking it out in trials and hardships that work gets done in our lives. As the sermon to Hebrews insists, we endure hardship as discipline, following the example set by Christ's endurance on the cross (12:1–7). Keeping the reward of it in focus, "we are not of those who shrink back and are destroyed, but of those who believe and are saved" (10:32–39).

With reference to Ecclesiasticus 2:4–5 and the declaration that patience is necessary for the daily bodily torments of sickness and loss, Cyprian asserts that there is nothing to "distinguish between the unrighteous and the righteous more, than that in affliction the unrighteous man impatiently complains and blasphemes, while the righteous is proved by his patience."[8]

This makes sense if Michael Casey is right to say that patience is the "real battleground where the reality of our *faith* is tested."

5. Kardong, *Benedict's Rule*, 4 (from the Prologue).

6. Kardong, *Benedict's Rule*, 20.

7. Hauerwas, *Hannah's Child*, 274.

8. Cyprian, "Patience," 17.

He is right to argue that failure in faith is not so much something that has to do with creed as it has to do with throwing ourselves on God's providence, believing that "God is acting for our salvation through the events that constitute the daily grind."[9]

Throwing ourselves on God's providence is an act of patient submission, but Ogliari reminds us that this submission "has nothing to do with that false indifference, synonym of selfishness, that some people assume before injustices or sufferings perpetrated against their neighbor." This is so because such patient submission is "ultimately based on faith and nourished by the certainty that God's kingdom grows and advances in the midst of opposition, humiliations and contradictions, . . . and even in those events where the divine essence seems to be absent." So we "hold on to God by fighting, so to say, that 'profusion of death' that attempts to expand its influence into the sphere of our life by undermining the tenacity and transparency of our faith in him."[10]

The kind of holding on to God by fighting that is characteristic of patience is described well by Robert Fitch when, writing on the theme of love and suffering, he asserts that "Patience is not mere passivity. . . . Patience is the power of those who, having given all they can of their own toward the furthering of the good, have confidence that providence in its own time will bring things to fulfillment."[11]

One of the most amazing instances of such patience that was empowered by faith in God's providence was the Montgomery Bus Boycott during the days of overt racial segregation in the US.

The boycott began on December 5, 1955, after Rosa Parks refused to move to the back of the bus from the middle section that was designated for whites if no more seating was available in the "white only" section.[12] To say that the boycott was a hardship

9. Casey, *Balaam's Donkey*, 315.

10. Ogliari, *"Laus Patientiae,"* 14.

11. Fitch, *Of Love and Suffering*, 56.

12. The first who was arrested for refusing to move was actually a fifteen-year-old named Claudette Colvin in an incident that took place nine months earlier. Colvin became one of the original five litigants in *Browder v. Gayle* that

on the majority of riders who were black is an understatement, as Taylor Branch's account makes clear:

> As for the boycotters themselves, the religious fervor they went to bed with at night always congealed by the next morning into cold practicality, as they faced rainstorms, mechanical breakdowns, stranded relatives, and complicated relays in getting from home to job without being late or getting fired or getting into an argument with the employer, then getting home again, perhaps having to find a way to and from the grocery store, and cooking and eating supper, dealing with children and housework, then perhaps going back out into the night for a mass meeting and finally home again, recharged by the "rousements" of Abernathy and the inspiration of King, and then at last some weary but contented sleep before the aching chill of dawn started the cycle all over again. To a largely uneducated people among whom the most common occupations were maid and day laborer, the loss of what was for many their most important modern convenience—cheap bus transportation—left them with staggering problems of logistics and morale.[13]

It didn't help that Montgomery police stopped carpool drivers for the slightest infractions—even for going too slow. Traffic fines diverted money from the MIA (Montgomery Improvement Association) carpool fund to the city treasury, and drivers worried that auto insurance would be canceled, or licenses suspended. But still they persevered. They continued to do so knowing that the two-to-one June 4 vote in their favor by a federal court in a suit that had been filed in February was appealed to the US Supreme Court by the state of Alabama. As Branch put it, "Optimism broke out like an epidemic. Every hardship, every funeral of a faithful walker who had died, became grist for inspiration to keep walking

---

eventually ended Montgomery bus segregation. But black leaders did not rally around Colvin as they did Rosa Parks because the unmarried teenager was reportedly impregnated by a married man. See Hoose, *Claudette Colvin*.

13. Branch, *Parting the Waters*, 145.

another six months if necessary. Everybody knew that the first six months had been the hard ones."[14]

Once the Supreme Court declared Alabama's state and local laws requiring segregation on buses to be unconstitutional (without even listening to an argument!), legal technicalities delayed the implementation. The snail pace of paperwork by the court lasted for five more weeks.

> This meant that during the interim, bus segregation remained the law and the MIA could provide no alternative transportation system. To endure this delay without provoking the whites to legal harassments, MIA leaders summoned up the last reserves of energy within their followers to keep boycotting the buses until the integration orders arrived. They would walk. In effect, they would struggle through a victory lap.[15]

In the meantime, Martin Luther King Jr. delivered a speech nearly a year from the time he had inspired the boycott with an address that put him on the map. In the speech he made it clear that the year had taught the participants that they could stick together for a common cause without selling out, that they had gained a new sense of dignity and destiny, and that they had employed the weapon of nonviolent resistance against threats and violence that had been meant to intimidate them.[16] Then, seventeen days later, on December 20, 1956, US Marshalls served notice on city officials to implement the Supreme Court's decision, and King announced that the walking was over. The creative activity of patience had won out.

Quoting Lewis Smedes along the way, Donald Bloesch's words captures the essence of the patience displayed in the bus boycott:

> Long-suffering does not counsel resignation to evil but enables one to hold evil in check. It implies not the acceptance of injustice but the willingness to suffer injustice. Lewis Smedes here resonates with biblical teaching:

14. Branch, *Parting the Waters*, 188.
15. Branch, *Parting the Waters*, 194.
16. Branch, *Parting the Waters*, 195.

"Longsuffering . . . is the power to be a creative victim. Longsuffering is not passive. It is a tough, active, aggressive style of life." Long-suffering is walking through the valley of the shadow of death in the knowledge that God is in control of all things and that the people of God have the promise that nothing can separate them from God's love (Rom. 8:37–39). . . . [This] is not drifting but enduring and overcoming. It is not procrastination but waiting . . . seeing the hand of God in the most dire circumstances and rejoicing in the victory of God, which is already in effect through the cross and resurrection of Jesus Christ.[17]

It is not only our faith that is tested in situations such as the bus boycott. There *are* situations in which God calls us to works of justice. But other times God may also call us to acts of mercy. And at those times our *love* is tested as well. Tertullian made the connection with some hermeneutical gymnastics, arguing that before Christ, impatience enjoyed opportunities the law gave—eye for an eye, tooth for a tooth, evil for evil. But Christ "united faith with patience," so that anger and revenge is prohibited; instead, we are commanded to love our enemies (Matt 5:44–45): "In this principal precept the universal discipline of patience is succinctly comprised, since evil-doing is not conceded even when it is deserved."[18]

Patience is characteristic of love. It's the first one on the list! (1 Cor 13:4). Patience makes love possible when it is difficult to love. So Tertullian takes it even further, outlining how Paul's descriptions of love in 1 Corinthians 13 are "taught" by patience: "For by whose teachings but those of Patience is Charity . . . trained." So patient love is long-suffering, beneficent, not envious, savors no violence, does not seek her own advantage, and is not irritable. "'Charity endures all things; tolerates all things;' of course because

17. Bloesch, *Pursuit of Holiness*, 56. Also, see Bloesch, *Spirituality*, 77–79. In this treatment of "long-suffering" he unpacks the examples of Job, Francis of Assisi, John of the Cross, Teresa of Avila, John Calvin, Martin Luther, Charles Spurgeon, P. T. Forsyth, and Martin Luther King Jr., who "succeeded because his attention was focused on the living God whose will is invincible, but it is the invincibility of love."

18. Tertullian, "Patience," 6.

she is patient. Justly then, 'will she never fail'; for all other things will be cancelled, will have their end.'"[19]

Cyprian concurred, citing 1 Corinthians 13:4–7 and Ephesians 4:2–3: "Take patience from love, and deprived of it love does not endure. Take from it the substance of bearing and of enduring, and it continues with no roots nor strength."[20]

With the Ephesians passage in mind, Cyprian went on to make the case that Paul "proved" that unity and peace among the church community required a love that practiced mutual toleration and "the intervention of patience." The necessity of patience for the exercise of love is also stressed by Benedict, as his Rule specifies how to live in close community with a variety of characters—the inevitable and unavoidable presence of the "other," not unlike the church in which we patiently bear with one another in love in order to grow up into the maturity measured by the full stature of Christ (Eph 4:2, 13). As one monk told me about God's call to join the abbey, "Monasticism means living with people you would not have chosen to live with if it had been up to you." This is made all the more significant by the vow of stability Benedictine monks take—to live with the same community for the rest of the monk's life, which is not unlike the vow married couples take. Indeed, Terrence Kardong's reflection on chapter 72 of the Benedictine Rule could apply to family life, let alone the monastic life to which Father Terrence refers. In this chapter on love Benedict urges the monks to "'support the physical and moral defects of one another with the greatest patience.' Hence the weaknesses of the individuals are seen as a unifying factor, because they need mutual help and forbearance." So the final sentence of the Rule's Prologue presents patience as "*the* doorway to the Kingdom of God. For cenobitic [i.e., communal] monks, committed to lifelong perseverance, patience means holding the course to the end."[21] Again, the lifetime project.

---

19. Tertullian, "Patience," 12.
20. Cyprian, "Patience," 15.
21. Kardong, *Benedict's Rule*, 25, italics in the original.

This gets specific in Benedict's instructions about caring for the sick (36.5). Though the sick are not to make excessive demands, the sick must be borne with patiently. So Kardong insists that patience is the overarching principle of this section of the Rule (chapter 36) in which the healthy are required to help bear the burden of the sick.[22] Again, the *weaknesses* of others becomes the *unifying* factor in a community that practices patient love.

In the context of learning patience in the midst of illness, Hauerwas and Pinches argue that it is precisely the community's presence that cultivates patience: "We have been given one another. To learn to live with the unavoidability of the other is to learn to be patient. Such patience comes not just from our inability to have the other do our will; more profoundly, it arises with the love that the presence of the other can and does create in us."[23]

But it is not just weaknesses and illnesses—the "daily bodily torments" as Cyprian calls them—for which patience is necessary. With Stephen, the church's first martyr and "the imitator of [Christ's] most patient gentleness," Cyprian has his model for the assertion that without "the steadfastness of patience and endurance" we cannot forgive, turn the other cheek, or forgive our enemies:

> What shall I say of anger, of discord, of strife, which things ought not to be found in a Christian? Let there be patience in our hearts, and these things cannot have a place there; or should they try to enter, they are quickly excluded and depart, that a peaceful abode may continue in the heart, where it delights the God of peace to dwell. . . . For if the Christian has taken leave of rage and worldly contention, just as one might hasten from a hurricane at sea, and has already begun to be tranquil and meek in the harbor of Christ, he ought to tolerate neither anger nor discord in his heart, since he must neither return evil for evil nor bear hatred toward another.[24]

---

22. Kardong, *Benedict's Rule*, 302.
23. Hauerwas and Pinches, "Practicing Patience," 176–77.
24. Cyprian, "Patience," 16.

Cyprian knows that the Christians of his era are eager to avenge persecutions from the Roman state, but, citing (among other passages) Zephaniah 3:8 and Revelation 6:9–11, where "Wait for the Lord" is the answer to the righteous who cry out "How long?," Cyprian maintains that refusing to return evil for evil and not bearing hatred requires patiently awaiting the day of God's vengeance and not hurrying to "revenge our suffering with an insolent haste."[25]

But not hurrying is not the same thing as aimlessness. As we have said, patience is not aimlessness. Patience is a characteristic of *hope*, just as it is an ingredient of faith and love. Theologically speaking, patience has an eschatological reference. As Paul put it to the Romans (8:24–25): "For in hope we were saved. . . . But if we hope for what we do not see, we wait for it with patience." With this passage in mind, Cyprian concluded, "Therefore, waiting and patience are needed, that we may fulfill that which we have begun to be, and may receive that which we believe and hope for."[26]

A former student and friend, Todd Billings, has written about this hope-filled patience from his perspective as one who is dying of incurable cancer. Citing Paul in Romans 8:23–25, Todd writes,

> We wait in hope, eagerly yet patiently. The "patience" of Paul here is not passivity but is closer to the sense of the English word "long-suffering." We cannot bring in God's kingdom ourselves. Our present bodies are decaying. . . . And yet our daily lives—our habits, our priorities, our willingness to take risks—are shaped by a durable hope for what is to come. We're called to long-suffering amid the trial we face, because we know—in hope—that *we* are not the ultimate solution to the world's ills. We are here to act in love and gratitude . . . . We are children of God in Christ. And yet this reality always looks forward—to the "hope of glory," the glorious hope of sharing in his resurrection, of sharing in the perfect communion that the Son has with the Father through the

---

25. Cyprian, "Patience," 21.
26. Cyprian, "Patience," 13.

Spirit. In our eager patience, we look to the hope of the restoration of the cosmos in and through Christ.[27]

As we have said, this kind of hopeful patience is not some "gritting your teeth" endurance, but the longing that *acts* out of hope, expressed beautifully in the life of Simeon (Luke 2:22–40), whose receptiveness has earned him the title *Theodochos* in Christian tradition—"God Receiver." Simeon responded to God's ancient promise of a Messiah by his daily "righteous and devout life," "looking forward," being guided by the Holy Spirit until, among all the parents and children whom he had seen come and go, he finally saw the one baby who was the salvation of Israel for which all had been waiting for centuries. Patient hope had come full circle. He held in his arms Yeshua ("the Lord is my salvation") who had come through the seed of Eve, descended as an offspring of Abraham in the line of David and Ruth, and now born of a peasant teenager named Mary. After centuries of waiting, Simeon can praise God, "Now you are dismissing your servant in peace."

For us who know how the story of Jesus unfolded, patience is expressive of the profound trust we have in a hoped-for future that has been guaranteed in the death, resurrection, and ascension of Jesus Christ. Those who persevere (*hypomone*) to the end—even as they are hated for their allegiance to Jesus—they will be saved, just as Jesus promised (Matt 10:22, 24:9–13; Mark 13:13; cf. 2 Tim 2:12; Jas 1:12). Or as Sonny put it in the movie *The Best Exotic Marigold Hotel*, "Everything will be alright in the end, so if it is not alright, it is not the end."

The end is coming, but when the Bible speaks about the "end," it is not talking about all of us leaving this earth, despite what some bumper stickers say. When the "end" comes, God's kingdom will be established once and for all in *this* world he created, with the Creator at the center once again, except that this time nothing will defeat righteousness—nothing will ruin the right relationships God has intended for us and his creation (Rom 8:35–39).

---

27. Billings, *Christian Life*, 19.

But even when discussing the end, Paul reminds us we aren't there yet. In this in-between time, Paul reminds us that the "creation was subjected to futility," emptiness, frustration; it is in "bondage to decay," corruption, ruin, deterioration. The "whole creation groans in pain. . . . and not only the creation, but we ourselves, who have the first fruits of the Spirit, groan inwardly while we wait for adoption, the redemption of our bodies" (Rom 8:20–23).

All of us suffer the futility and decay that all of creation was subjected to in Genesis 3 and from which it will be released according to the vision in Revelation 22. We suffer loneliness, or betrayal from family and friends, or the triumph of an enemy, or powerlessness against diseases like cancer, or the deterioration of old age, or the death of a loved one, or the loss of a job, or the barrenness that leaves a couple childless, or discrimination because of differences of melanin.

Even when we seem to be doing all the right things, we are frustrated. I once heard a story attributed to the great industrialist Armand Hammer, who responded to a young woman who asked him why he was in such good shape given the fact that he was over eighty years old. He told her that he didn't smoke, didn't drink hard liquor, and swam a half-hour every day. The young woman in turn responded that her father didn't smoke or drink and exercised every day, yet he died at fifty-seven. "What did he do wrong?" she asked. Hammer answered: "He didn't do it long enough!" Indeed, not one of us will "do it long enough." If no other great tragedy interrupts our lives, all of us are in bondage to decay and death, says the apostle Paul. Some of us even experience daily the frustration in the more mundane events of life, such as the urban traffic that leads some to take out their frustration with violent means.

All of our earthly projects and prospects are subject to corruption, to frustration, to disappointment—even our attempts to forge peace in the world, to overcome racism, to wipe out disease, to feed the hungry, to stop terrorism, to construct the perfect family, to be the most successful we can be at our profession.

Paul is right! The *whole* creation is in bondage to futility, to corruption. Nothing and no one is exempt. Even the Christian experiences the full force of this futility and decay. We, too, suffer. Weeds grow in the believer's garden just as much as they grow in the unbeliever's garden.

Yet, we do not leave it there. If our prospects for the future were only a constant battle with the weeds, then the proper response would be just to tolerate our lives or to grit our teeth and stoically resign ourselves to it or to be an eternal pessimist. But the Christian, the one in whom the love of God is poured out, the one in whom the Spirit says "You are a child of God"—that one is not led to despair, but to hope. The Christian is the one who suspects that this futility is not the last word! She is the one who anticipates a future glorious existence of justice, freedom, peace, and joy that cannot even be compared to the present sufferings.

The words that Paul uses to describe our anticipation of the future conjure up a strong image (Rom 8:22–23). Paul describes creation as suffering in agony. He describes both creation and the Christian as *groaning* or *sighing* together. This groaning is precisely due to the *hope* that we have in the midst of the pain and suffering. It is not merely groaning under the decay of the present, but groaning *for* the glory to be revealed. This is not the groaning of one who is dying, but of one who is giving birth. These are not the death pangs of those who live without hope; these are the birth pangs of those who anticipate a renewed heaven and a renewed earth. The entire creation is a symphony of sighs. We could say that such sighs and groaning is another manifestation of our patience.

We groan for the day when our redemption will be completed—when we will finally share in God's glory, not as spectators, but as *active participants* who mirror his image perfectly because in this in-between time we will have been perfectly conformed to his likeness. We will be in every sense of the word the sons and daughters of God.

To be sure, even if we are not groaning, there is at least in all of us a subconscious awareness that things should be better than they are—that the world isn't supposed to work like this.

The saying "Hope springs eternal" refers to a deep-seated optimism in human beings. We are so optimistic that we believe in the evolutionary progress of the human race despite the fact that we continue to commit some of the worst atrocities of any species on the planet. Deep down inside, all of us hope for a new heaven and a new earth—the rescue of God's creation. The whole creation participates in this on a subconscious level, as Paul implies.

And there's the rub. Even the optimism, let alone *bona fide* Christian hope, requires that we *wait*. And the groaning that accompanies waiting often comes not out of any Christian hope, but more often out of pagan impatience. We just do not like to wait. It is *hard* to be a patient "hoper"—to hope for what God is going to do in us and to us and for our world while we suffer in the meantime. We're like the Hebrews in Exodus who want to go back to Egypt rather than suffer the hardships they will have to endure in order to get to the promised land.

But the New Testament makes it clear time and time again that *patient suffering precedes glory*. Admittedly, that is not attractive to our modern ears, for with all or our technological know-how we like to think that we are in control and that we should alleviate our suffering or bypass it. As a result we have become weak in character. It has been said that with our technology we are capable of doing anything except for one thing—we have lost the ability to suffer well.

Remember those times when you were a little kid sitting in the back seat of the car headed for Disneyland or the beach or the mountains, badgering Mom and Dad with the question, "Are we there yet?" And the longer you rode, the more you wanted to arrive. It's that way with our lives. We want peace and justice and all the bad things to go away, and we have been promised this. The longer the journey takes the more our anticipation of God's promised future increases, especially as we experience the continuing wars and loneliness and illnesses of life. We are stretched thin, and so we find ourselves crying out to God, "Lord, are we there yet?!" or with the psalmist, "How long?!"

So patience is exercised when we do not immediately reach our goal, something that Abraham had to cultivate in light of all that the covenanting God promised (Heb 6:11–15). It was exercised by Israel as she often questioned God, "How long?" (Jer 14:8; Ps 130:5–8). And Christ's resurrection and our future resurrection led Tertullian to advise those whose family and friends had died to reckon as needless the "impatience of grief" and, instead, to long for the lost one rather than lament the lost one, tempering the longing with patience.[28]

Sometimes it is fear that makes waiting difficult. We want to flee or fight out of fear, and the more afraid we are, the harder it is to wait. This is why hope requires the assurance that God loves us. As Henri Nouwen reminds us, all the figures on the first pages of Luke's Gospel are waiting as representatives of Israel who have been encouraged not to fear because God has something good in store for them. They wait attentively, expectantly, with a sense of promise. Waiting is like the seed that is already growing, not dug up: "We can only really wait if what we are waiting for has already begun for us. . . . It's always a movement from something to something more." That something more is the coming kingdom in its fullness.[29]

As we anticipate the something more, Stanley Hauerwas argues that our hope for the complete fulfillment of the kingdom of God must be *schooled by patience* lest our hope turn into fanaticism on the one hand or cynicism on the other. We live between the times as the church of the new age existing in the old age—an age that often relies on coercion and violence to achieve its ends. And so patience "is one of the most needed virtues, if we are to live amid this violent world as peaceable people." Especially in the face of suffering and injustice we live as eschatological people who believe that God will use our faithfulness to make the kingdom a reality. This is not acquiescence to injustice nor even mere self-preservation, but patient hopeful confidence that God's kingdom virtues must dictate our active resistance.[30]

28. Tertullian, "Patience," 9.
29. Nouwen, *Finding My Way Home*, 114.
30. Hauerwas, *Peaceable Kingdom*, 103–6.

Michael Casey concurs: "Without such a vision, suffering is meaningless. . . . Without such an eschatological perspective patience is impossible . . . . Patience is the sum of Christian praxis. The kingdom of God is such a rich gift that it superabundantly compensates for the loss of goods or the need to endure the effect of evil."[31]

So hope makes patience necessary if we are to avoid the worldly illusion that brute force is the means to God's ends or if we are not to succumb to resigned passivity. To that point, Episcopal priest and theologian Fleming Rutledge says that the church's calling is both active resistance and patient endurance. But the way she proceeds to describe active resistance against evil makes it even more reliant on patient endurance. For the manner in which the church wages war is in "the nature more of 'take up your cross' (Mark 8:34) than of 'take up your sword,' let alone 'take up your AK-47.'" Referring to Paul's imperative to take up the "armor of light" (Rom 13:12), Rutledge reminds us that this has to do with life in the Spirit (Rom 8:5), not anything having to do with the "flesh," such as bullet proof vests, cruise missiles, nuclear submarines, or anything else belonging to the enemy's territory.[32]

So, hope-filled patience is *creatively and imaginatively active*. Princeton theologian Daniel Migliore expresses this best:

> Christians truly learn the meaning of hope in the grace of God only in the practices of discipleship. . . . As the church waits and prays, it also acts. Christian hope . . . does not immobilize people, but makes them eager to get to work. It is not escapist hope, but creative hope. It seeks for provisional manifestations, anticipatory realizations of God's new world of justice and peace. [But] we are also reminded, personally and corporately, of the incompleteness of these victories. . . . [So] Christians are to proclaim the gospel and work with imagination and energy for the realization of many "little hopes." . . . In reliance on the "God of hope" (Rom 15:13), Christians dare to persevere in a life of service and costly discipleship when others have given up the task as hopeless. Christians struggle

---

31. Casey, *Living in the Truth*, 118, 123–24.
32. Rutledge, "When God Is Silent," 211–12.

against apathy and resignation to plant seeds of hope and new life. The call to hope, even and especially in the darkest hour, is beautifully expressed in the statement attributed to Luther: "If I knew tomorrow that the world would end I would still plant an apple tree today."[33]

But Migliore also reminds us that there are no guarantees. "Christian hope offers no guarantee of quick or easy success. It remembers that Christ was crucified. True hope is thus learned only as it is practiced in companionship with the crucified Christ and those whose suffering he shares. Only in that location is it possible to discover that God's grace is sufficient."[34] *The cruciform patience we have discussed unfolds in the creative activity sustained by hope.*

---

33. Migliore, *Faith Seeking Understanding*, 371–72.
34. Migliore, *Faith Seeking Understanding*, 372.

6

Waiting on God

WHILE SIFTING THROUGH THE Psalms one day I began to notice that the phrase "wait on God" was repeated over and over. The theme occurs in no fewer than twelve psalms, depending on how you count. It first hit me when I read Psalm 37: "Be still before the Lord, and wait patiently for him; do not fret over those who prosper in their way, over those who carry out evil devices" (v. 7); "Wait for the Lord, and keep to his way, and he will exalt you to inherit the land; you will look on the destruction of the wicked" (v. 34). The Hebrew verb *qwh* translated "wait" shows up twenty times in the Psalms, occasionally rendered "to tarry" or "to hope." The sentiment is perhaps expressed best in Psalm 40, often put to contemporary music, most notably by U2 in a song simply entitled "40" that reiterates the refrain, "How long?"

Even though Psalm 40 restates the psalmist's trust in the Lord and the "new song" that God has given the psalmist, his concern over God's apparent delay constantly slices through the confidence: "I waited patiently for the Lord" (v. 1); "Do not, O Lord, withhold your mercy from me" (v. 11); "Be pleased, O Lord, to deliver me; O Lord, make haste to help me" (v. 13); ending with the plea, "do not delay, O my God" (v. 17).

In Psalm 25:3, the psalmist begs God not to let those who wait for God be shamed in the presence of those who violently hate the psalmist. In a similar vein, Proverbs 20:22 instructs us to wait for the Lord when we are tempted to seek revenge. By the time we get to the latter prophets and writings (*qwh* does not appear in the former prophets), Isaiah (51:5), Jeremiah (14:22), and Hosea (12:6) express the attitude of Israel as she waits in exile with hope-filled "strength and courage from the certainty of what is yet to be."[1] But under present circumstances in exile, waiting on God while others "prosper in their way" and "carry out evil desires" does not seem to be wise advice. It seems to be naïve.

Indeed, the confidence expressed by the psalmist and by the latter prophets is not always experienced by those who profess faith in Yahweh. Per word count, Psalm 130 expresses the waiting and hoping on God more than any other Psalm: "Out of the depths I cry to you, O Lord. Lord, hear my voice! . . . I wait for the Lord, my soul waits, and in his word I hope; my soul waits for the Lord . . . O Israel, hope in the Lord!" It is particularly significant, then—or, as John Goldingay put it, ironical—that Psalm 130 was inscribed on a chapel wall at Dachau, "where the depths indeed stand for the depths of death and for a waiting that sees no response."[2] More than naïve, waiting for God in such circumstances seems ludicrous.

Surely the experience of many at Dachau was a waiting that knew only the silence of God. God's silence is a biblical theme related to that of waiting on God that appears in the Psalms and latter prophets in the experience of Israel's exile. And among our contemporaries, waiting on a silent God is not only the horrendous experience of those in a Nazi concentration camp; it is the universal experience in moments of tragedy or despair when we cry out to God, but God does not seem present or concerned. There is perhaps no more significant expression of this than Jesus' cry of dereliction on the cross as he utters the first words of Psalm 22.

---

1. Mays, *Psalms*, 407.
2. Goldingay, *Psalms, Vol. 3*, 529.

In her sermon entitled "The Silence of God," Barbara Brown Taylor brings this home with poignancy.[3] The physical pain of the cross was not as bad as what others have endured, and certainly it was more painful for Jesus to bear the betrayal and desertion of his intimate friends. But, says Taylor, "The worst is the silence of God. The God who does not act. The God who is not there. The God who—by a single word—could have made all the pain bearable but did not speak, not so Jesus could hear, anyway. The only voice at the end was his own, screaming his last, unanswered question at the sky." What is even more confusing for us is that the voice from heaven had confirmed Jesus twice before, in his baptism and transfiguration. She asks, why not once more? "What a difference it would have made. A confirmation like that, a blessing on the destitute moment at hand. But it did not come and Jesus died alone, having pronounced himself abandoned by God." And now, she tells us, such divine silence is what every believer must face when he or she cries out for protection, rescue, a way out. Taylor goes on to affirm that, while we have no choice but to go through the suffering, we are allowed to hate it and do what we can to bring it to an end, and we must be assured that, despite appearances, we are not left with defeat, but with a God who protests against the pain when God's people cry out.[4]

To be clear, God's silence is not the experience of those who are indifferent to religion, but of those who are genuine believers. The seeming absence of a benevolent and almighty God in a

3. See Taylor, "Silence of God," 112–14, for what follows.

4. She cites Shusaku Endo's novel *Silence*, and then reflects: "When Jesus howls his last question on the cross, it is God who howls—protesting the pain, opposing it with his last breath. Only this is no defeat. This is, contrary to all appearances, a triumph over suffering. By refusing to avoid it or to lie about it in any way, the crucified one opens a way through it.

"He hallows it by engaging it. He shows us how. We are not supposed to love suffering. We are allowed to hate it and to do everything in our power to bring it to an end, only we may not avoid it. That is not one of our choices. Today we look on the one whom we have pierced. More important, we listen. To the silence. To the howl. What is the gospel, in the land at the foot of the cross? When God is silent, people of faith cry out. When people of faith cry out, it is God who speaks. Amen." Taylor, "Silence of God," 114.

world filled with horrendous evils has led many to insist on God's irrelevance. But then they are no longer speaking about the silence *of* God in the same sense that a true believer like Habakkuk did when he pled, "O Lord, how long shall I cry for help, and you will not listen? Or cry to you 'Violence!' and you will not save?" (1:2) God seemed silent when God did not immediately save and judge in the midst of evil (Pss 22, 35, 50, 83, 109: Hab 1:1–2, 13; Isa 65:6; cf. Job 23:8–9). In other words, the believer's pleas are not uttered as if one were knocking on the door of an empty house or talking on one's phone to a nonentity on the other end.

In a sermon that works off of Isaiah's assertion that God is a God who hides himself (45:15), Fleming Rutledge insists that the silence and absence of God is a major theme of Scripture and the Christian life. The people of the Bible ask where God is when terrible things happen, and one has a shallow faith if she does *not* ask such questions.[5] So this experience of waiting for a God who remains silent is an aspect of mature Christian faith.

Karl Rahner contended that even though God has always been felt to be incomprehensible and remote, we moderns experience this with a "new and radical keenness" because the world is more vast and more profane than ever before, and God seems no longer to be found in the realm of everyday experiences. He wrote, "God is, to a large extent, experienced as the silent mystery, infinite in his ineffability and inconceivability. And the more man advances in his religious life the more *these* aspects of God come consistently to the fore (instead of diminishing)."[6]

Of course, some of this is on God, since at times God means to be silent or hidden for God's own reasons, just as God speaks or shows up for God's own reasons.[7]

What the psalmist fears is that this silence of God is permanent—that it is the deathlike stillness and deathlike darkness of those who are in the grave (Pss 94:17, 115:17). But, despite this

---

5. Rutledge, "When God Is Silent," 116.

6. Rahner, "Venerate the Saints?," 7.

7. Rutledge, "When God Is Silent," 119–20. Rutledge uses the phrase "presence-in-absence" to name the theme of God's self-disclosure.

fear, the believing psalmist is convinced that the silence is temporary, so that he waits on the God who will eventually act as Savior and Judge. When God's silence *does* end and God responds to human cries, God vindicates himself and God's people over against wickedness, disobedience, and idolatry, as in God's declaration in Psalm 65:6: "I will not keep silent, but I will repay."

So we have assurance that waiting on God does not imply God's absence, death, irrelevance, or indifference. In fact, in one sense it can be an invitation to enter into a deeper relationship with God. And God's silence may speak louder than words. There is a prime example of this in Matthew's account of the Canaanite woman's encounter with Jesus.

As Matthew tells the story (15:21-28), the woman was a Canaanite—not only a gentile, but from the stock of the Jews' enemies. She was also a mother—the mother of a very sick little girl who was tormented by a demonic and destructive force. And here, coming into gentile territory, was Jesus that Jewish miracle-worker she had probably heard so much about—the one whose acts of compassion and healing had been talked about far and wide. So, out of her desperate and real need—not unlike us when our child is terribly ill, we are in financial trouble, or our marriage is falling apart—she cried out seeking his help: "Have mercy on me, O Lord, Son of David; my daughter is severely possessed by a demon!" But Jesus did not answer her a word! Not one word! Just silence! The only answer—as some of us have experienced—was the echo of her own pleading voice.

The disciples misinterpret Jesus' silence as indifference to the woman's plight, urging Jesus to send this nuisance away. This misinterpretation is not without precedence, even in our times, as we have said.

There are other possible interpretations of God's silence, some of which are theologically legitimate. For instance, in the presence of evil or injustice, sometimes God does not get even; God just gets out. And that silence speaks louder than words. We know that silence can communicate displeasure in response to an obscene or inappropriate remark, leaving the guilty party's words ringing over and over. Certainly this seems to be God's intention in response to one of Israel's tribes when God told Hosea, "Ephraim is joined to idols. Let him alone" (Hos 4:17). And, with divine consistency, the same is affirmed in the first chapter of Paul's Letter to the Romans. Three times in less than ten verses Paul describes the manner in which God's wrath is revealed against the ungodliness and wickedness of those who know him through his creation yet refuse to acknowledge this truth: God *gave them up* to their own impurity and passions (Rom 1:24, 26, 28). God's judgment does not always come in lightning bolts of revenge; in silent absence God leaves us to our own self-destructive sinful activity. God does not get even. God just gets out.

Of course, there are times when God is not silent. At times, we simply refuse to hear what God is saying. We often blame God at such times, even with pious thoughts that God is testing our faith by God's silence while we are patient enough to endure it.

For instance, maybe a person is angry at God because God seems to be silent in the midst of the problems one is having in her business, when the real fault is hers for not hearing what God has already told her in Scripture about conducting business affairs with integrity or being more concerned about the employees or the people whom the business serves than about the money made. Maybe a husband is blaming God for being silent while his marriage falls apart, when he hasn't ever really listened to what God has already told him in Scripture about genuine love that never demands its own way but always considers the other person as more important. The problem is not that God is silent. The problem is that we are often not patiently quiet long enough to hear what God is saying to us, instead hearing only what *we* want to hear.

I believe that this helps us to explain Jesus' silence in the story of the Canaanite woman. Jesus was preoccupied with his own agenda—with the demands placed upon him by his mission to the people of Israel. And he does not answer the gentile woman's plea for her daughter until he is sure that she has understood his mission to Israel and how her needs fit into God's agenda. That explains all that talk about children's bread and dog's crumbs.[8] By Jesus' initial silence and his subsequent response, he was able to draw her out of her own concerns to see God's concerns—to see how *her* situation fit into God's plans rather than to impatiently demand that God fit into her plans.

Obviously, the Canaanite woman believed that Jesus' silence was not a dead-end silence, but a silence that invited her to come closer, to kneel, and to keep on pleading. It was a silence that drew out her faith, a faith that sustained her pleading even when it was at first not answered, even when the disciples spurned her, and even when Jesus tested her motives. It was a silence that was eventually broken with the words: "O woman, great is your faith. Be it done for you as you desire."

The woman was encouraged to see how her request needed to fit into Jesus' agenda rather than the other way around. By his initial silence, Jesus gave her space to do just that. That patient silence gave her the opportunity to respond with her remark that even the dogs—even the gentiles—get crumbs that fall from the table of the children—Israel's feast.

In a sense, unlike the disciples' impatient encouragement to reprimand the noisy woman, the woman was given an opportunity to wait on God—to exercise an active and creative patience that drew her even closer in body and mind to the One who eventually answered her plea.

What the Canaanite woman realized is that Jesus reveals a God of infinite possibilities when we humans are only aware of our finite limitations. Time and again in Israel's literature there are expressions of seemingly pointless waiting—for justice, for peace, for comfort (e.g., Isa 5:7, 59:9–11; Jer 8:15, 14:19; Ps 69:20; Job 3:9). Yet, much as the Canaanite woman discovered in her encounter with the initial silence of Jesus that drew her in, as Daniel Schibler puts it, "Hope and expectant waiting on God are most often expressed when humans are particularly aware of their finiteness and God's infiniteness. . . . Hope and expectant waiting are linked

---

8. There are those who suggest that in Jesus' kenotic humanity he responds inappropriately at first before learning to empathize with the woman's plea.

to people's need to draw upon God's resources, especially when confronted with the question of goals in life."[9] We hear this in the psalmist's recognition that a lifetime is but a few breaths and nothing in God's sight, yet he rhetorically asks, "O Lord, what do I wait for?" and immediately answers, "My hope is in you" (Ps 39:4–7).

This response of the psalmist must be seen in the context of Israel's expectation—even in exile—that God, the "hope of Israel," will keep the covenant promises made to her (Jer 14:8, 17:13, 29:11, 31:17). Again, as Schibler puts it, "the psalmists [and we could add the latter prophets] have an audacious certainty about them that seems to be substantiated by nothing but God."[10]

As John Goldingay notes, the very word *qwh* implies a recognition that we have little control over our lives, whether it's recovering from an illness or managing our political destiny; yet, that is an aspect of the waiting this Hebrew verb connotes, since Israel's vocation is "to live in the expectation that Yhwh is going to act and to live straining its eyes to see that act." The verb implies a posture of *looking* for something to happen, *looking* for Yhwh to act. (Again, recall Ps 130:5–6.)[11]

So waiting on God is *active* in the sense that we strain to *see* God act. Such waiting for or on God is like waiting at an airport terminal for your ride to show up or sitting in a restaurant booth waiting for the other party to arrive. It's an attentive looking . . . while one is waiting—praying. "Be still . . . look . . ."

In her own way, philosopher and mystic Simone Weil captures this aspect of the Hebrew *qwh* in her discussion of the act of "attention." She says, "Attention is an effort, the greatest of all efforts perhaps, but it is a negative effort." By "negative effort" she means that it is receptive, "ready to be penetrated by the object." She suggests that such attentive waiting is not the same thing as searching for. Perhaps in resonance with Goldingay's comment about Israel's vocation of living in expectation that Yhwh will act rather than trying to control what we cannot, Weil says that "this

9. Schibler, *Qwh*, 894.

10. Schibler, *Qwh*, 895.

11. Goldingay, *Psalms, Vol. 3*, 529.

way of looking is first of all attentive. The soul empties itself of its own contents in order to receive into itself the being it is looking at [or for], just as he is, in all his truth."[12] Later, she argues that this effort of looking—much like the kind of effort with which a fiancée accepts her lover in an act of attention and consent—is the effort that brings a soul to salvation, just as it did when the bronze serpent was lifted up "so that those who lay maimed in the depths of degradation should be saved by looking upon it."[13]

In his own way, Michael Casey concurs with Weil. He writes,

> What powers patience is a progressive switch in the focus of consciousness. . . . The quiet mind of patience results from the action of grace at a deep level that eludes our immediate awareness. . . . Our task is to wait in hope. There is no other way to union with God. . . . The sufferings that come unbidden to one who has embarked on the spiritual ascent cannot be understood. There is a saving grace in this unknowing. . . . The gifts of grace surpass human discernment. As long as we are bound to our own powers of assessment, no room is left for the God of surprises.[14]

What Weil and Casey are getting at has implications for social justice. Weil's sense of the "negative effort" of the creative work of attention is developed in her discussion of the parable of the Good Samaritan.[15] Those who pass by this "thing" scarcely notice it.

> Only one stops and turns his attention toward it. The actions that follow are just the automatic effort of this moment of attention. The attention is creative. But at the moment when it is engaged it is a renunciation. . . . The man accepts to be diminished by concentrating on an expenditure of energy, which will not extend his own power

12. Weil, *Waiting for God*, 61, 62, 65.

13. Weil, *Waiting for God*, 125–26.

14. Casey, *Living in the Truth*, 120–22.

15. See Weil, *Waiting for God*, 91–95 for what follows. As someone has noted, continuing to use "good" with "Samaritan" has unfortunate implications about Samaritans, as if we *have* to add the adjective. But it's difficult to refer to this parable in any other way since the precedent has been set.

> but will only give existence to a being other than himself,
> who will exist independently of him. . . . Creative atten-
> tion means really giving our attention to what does not
> exist. Humanity does not exist in the anonymous flesh
> lying inert by the roadside. The Samaritan who stops
> and looks gives his attention all the same to this absent
> humanity, and the actions which follow prove that it is a
> question of real attention.

This "affliction,"—which for Weil refers to the "destruction of oneself"—this denial of oneself on the part of the Samaritan, involves
his submersion into the life of the other as he recognizes with love
what is invisible. So Weil concludes, "Justice in punishment can be
defined in the same way as justice in almsgiving. It means giving
our attention to the victim of affliction as to a being and not a thing;
it means wishing to preserve in him the faculty of free consent."

Again, waiting for and looking for the person who is meeting
you for lunch engages one's attention in the same manner that Weil
describes. It takes the focus off of oneself and fixes it on the one
who is to come. In the same way, waiting for and looking for God
in the sense of the Hebrew verb *qwh* redirects our attention from
self to the One to whom we plead for justice and salvation. And
given that that One is the Creator of the universe, we acquiesce to
that One's "free consent" to do when and how God wishes. That
doesn't make our waiting any easier, any more than my three-hour
stressful wait for a ride at the Duluth airport one very cold winter
day while suffering a life-defying cold. Granted, I was not unaware
of my own existence, but my attention *was* centered on my hope
for the arrival of the Benedictine Sister who would be an instrument of temporary salvation, just as Israel pleaded "How long?!"
with the One who would deliver God's people from exile.

We have established that patience is creative activity, but
here this must be nuanced. In his commentary on Psalm 37:34,
Goldingay says that waiting on the Lord and looking for the destruction of the wicked does not imply *inactivity*, but activity that
is "not an attempt to seize control of one's destiny but an attempt

to keep Yhwh's way, in the conviction that Yhwh is keeping our way (v. 28)."[16] The faithful who are distraught at the injustice they experience are to look for the destruction of the wicked based on what they have seen Yhwh do in the past: "They are inclined to fret at the fact that wrongdoers do well in life—maybe better than the faithful. Indeed the faithless are a threat to the faithful: they scheme against them. The faithless are the strong, the faithful the weak. In that situation, the preacher wants the faithful to drop anger and rather to trust Yhwh, delight in Yhwh, commit things to Yhwh, be still before Yhwh, wait for Yhwh."[17]

Israel must expect God to act and, as Goldingay puts it, "strain its eyes to see that act." Such patient waiting is an expression of trust and implies a willingness to submit to Yhwh, rather than succumb to agitation and anger, especially in the context of the unjust who are successful in worldly terms. Or, in the psalmist's words: "When you are disturbed, do not sin; ponder it on your beds, and be silent" (4:4). "For God alone my soul waits in silence, for my hope is in him."[18]

A graphic portrayal of the psalmist's sentiments occurs in the sermon of Pastor Julius von Jan, preached on the Sunday after *Kristallnacht*. The day after he preached this sermon on Jeremiah's cry for justice and warning of God's wrath on unrepentant offenders, Julius von Jan was severely beaten by some five hundred Nazis, dragged to city hall, tried, and thrown into jail.[19] Calling for German repentance, he reflected, "We love so much to go our own ways. We are so busy with many things and take so little time for the silence in which we may hear the Lord's Word, ... That's why so many days pass without our having let God be our Lord, because in the morning we were not present to hear his orders. A Christian who fails to seek every morning this silence to hear God endangers himself and harms God's affairs."[20]

16. Goldingay, *Psalms, Vol. 1*, 531.
17. Goldingay, *Psalms, Vol. 1*, 533.
18. Goldingay, *Psalms, Vol. 1*, 522.
19. Jan, "O Land," 106.
20. Jan, "O Land," 113.

In this vein, Simone Weil, argued that "the great trouble in human life is that looking and eating are two different operations. . . . to eat what we should only look at. Eve began it."[21] In other words, for Weil the waiting and attention that remains constant (looking) through suffering (as well as joy) is nothing like muscular effort (eating). It is more like the paradigmatic act of obedience—the crucifixion of Christ. Sin is turning our gaze in the wrong direction, says Weil, and we have been doing this since the beginning and walking in the wrong direction as far as our gaze could go.[22]

The temptation in my three-hour wait at the Duluth airport was to expedite my transportation by finding a ride of my own making. (This was before the days of Uber and Lyft.) But that would be much like Israel's impatience that led her to worship a golden calf, instead of waiting for Moses to come down from the mountain. The failure to wait and look for God to act can devolve into idolatry.

Indeed, Habakkuk had to instruct his audience that God's silence is not to be confused with an idol—a "silent stone" (Hab 2:19–20), because the perennial temptation is impatience with God's silence that leads us to turn to idols—to have our god here and now, completely disposable at our discretion. Instead, Habakkuk urges the *believer* to keep silence before the Lord in his holy temple, for God *is* there, even if silent to our pleas for the moment. In order to resist the temptation to idolatry, the believer must maintain her faith in the God who is silent. For us, idolatry might be in the form of military might, guns, or political ideology—again, the "eating" rather than the "looking."

The biblical queries about God's silence typically include a confession of faith. There is the psalmist who implores God not to be silent while addressing God as "my rock" (28:1) and as the "God of my praise" (109:1). There is the continual confession of the suffering Job, epitomized in his affirmation, "Though he kill me, yet will I trust in him" (Job 13:15, alternative reading). Again,

---

21. Weil, *Waiting for God*, 105.
22. Weil, *Waiting for God*, 73.

the model for the believer's patience remains the crucified Christ who echoes the psalmist's "my God" at the moment when the crucified's attention is on the One who for an unexpressed reason remains silent.

This confession of faith is not some existential leap in the dark, but, as mentioned above, it is an *informed* faith—a faith informed by the remembrance of God's responses in the past. Habakkuk bemoans the fact that God has not heard his cries for help (1:2), yet he reminds himself of God's holy character (1:12–13) and on that basis waits for God's answer (2:1). The psalmist who wonders if God has forsaken him *immediately* (vv. 3–4) affirms, "Yet you are holy, enthroned on the praises of Israel. In you our ancestors trusted. They trusted, and you delivered them. To you they cried, and were saved; in you they trusted, and were not put to shame." And when God's silence ends and God does respond, faith is further informed and trust is strengthened (cf. Ps 28:1–2 with 28:6–7).

Indeed, what regularly informs our faith is Christ's suffering of God's silence on the cross and the subsequent vindication in the resurrection that we recall in the Eucharist. That is the mystery of faith: Christ has died. Christ is risen. Christ will come again.

Do we have some influence on God's decision to intervene, to break the silence, to speak and act in the midst of human suffering? G. B. Caird suggests so in relation to Revelation 8:1: "Just as the seals could not be broken until the Lamb had won the right to break them by his obedience on earth, so the trumpets cannot sound until the prayers of men have reached the altar of heaven."[23] Ultimately, however, it is God's choice. God is the One who remains silent if God wills to remain silent, and it is God who speaks when God wills for the vindication of himself and his people. The believer who at once affirms her belief in the existence of a benevolent and sovereign God—even in the occasional silence of that God in human experience—must maintain her historic faith even as she cries out in misery, "O God, do not keep silence!" It will take patience—the *hypomone* that Weil insists is "the waiting

23. Caird, *Revelation*, 107.

or attentive and faithful immobility [intense waiting for goodness and truth] that lasts indefinitely and cannot be shaken."[24]

Recalling the story of Simeon we encountered in chapter 5, if he lived another two years he heard news of Herod's orders to slaughter the male infants and toddlers in Bethlehem. This is the dark side of Christmas that goes beyond the charming Hallmark card prettiness and our "Santatizing" of the story. In fact, the church has for centuries marked off December 28 as the "Feast Day of Holy Innocents" so that we remember the wailing of mothers who would *not* be consoled two thousand years ago, just as surely as there are wailing mothers today in Israel and in Gaza and in Syria and in Ukraine and in Sudan who weep over the death of their little ones.

This is the wailing of all of us today who must still *wait*—who must be patient—for God to finish the work of the Genesis 3:15 promise that Eve's seed will crush the serpent's head—a promise that will be fulfilled through Jesus' birth, life, death, resurrection, and ascension. In the end, the hope and peace of Simeon is only made complete when the ascended Christ is recognized at last, and every knee bows and every tongue confesses that he is Lord.

But, we need to be reminded again that God is not in a hurry. God is patient. That does not stop us from asking why God took *so* long before he sent the "consolation of Israel" into our history as he had promised to Eve and Abraham and David and Isaiah. Why *is* God taking so long before God finishes bringing complete *shalom* to this world that rebelled against God so long ago and continues to express that rebellion in acts of injustice and hatred? We don't know.

What we *do* know is what we heard Tertullian assert in the first chapter: "Impatience is of the devil," for our impatience brings with it anger and hatred and revenge and, ultimately, despair. God's ways are not ours. God's time is not our time. The history of salvation is long. In the meantime, we either imitate the patience of God or the impatience of the devil.

24. Weil, *Waiting on God*, 128.

So in the interim we must struggle against evil in all its forms to remain faithful to God's vision of the kingdom. But to think that we can get rid of evil once and for all by our efforts is mistaken. That would be to take God's place and to reject the call not to fret—to wait on God. There may be no more profound biblical expression of this, *given* its social and economic context, than Micah's confession, "But as for me, I will *look* to the Lord, I will *wait* for the God of my salvation; my God *will* hear me." (7:7) Yes, it is waiting for a vision postponed in spite of all indications to the contrary. It is an eschatological hope so beautifully expressed in Isaiah (25:6–9):

> On this mountain the Lord of hosts will make for all peoples
> a feast of rich food, a feast of well-aged wines,
> of rich food filled with marrow, of well-aged wines strained clear.
> And he will destroy on this mountain
> the shroud that is cast over all peoples,
> the sheet that is spread over all nations;
> he will swallow up death forever.
> Then the Lord God will wipe away the tears from all faces,
> and the disgrace of his people he will take away from all the earth,
> for the Lord has spoken.
> It will be said on that day,
> Lo, this is our God; we have *waited* for him, so that he might save us.
> This is the Lord for whom we have *waited*;
> let us be glad and rejoice in his salvation.
> For the hand of the Lord will rest on this mountain.

7

Strategies

THE CHRISTIAN VIRTUE OF patience is not self-generated. It is first of all a gift of the Holy Spirit (Gal 5:22; Col 1:11). So gifted, we are commanded to make patience a way of life as we *walk* in the Spirit (Eph 4:2; Col 3:12). In other words, human intentionality follows from the giftedness.

Patience is necessary for accomplishing anything worthwhile. Those who attempt to master a Bach fugue on the organ or those who hunt ducks while sitting all day in a blind on a cold winter day know this. I am reminded of this when constructing a dollhouse for granddaughters and I am tempted to move to the next step before glue or paint is dry. Patience is also required for the worthwhile endeavor of character formation. In his edited volume, *Monastic Wisdom*, Hugh Feiss says, "Patience is essential, since the road to virtue is a long one. Only repeated effort and practice establish a habit, and a firm habit is frequently exercised. Especially at the beginning, the road is difficult."[1] But if patience is essential for cultivating a virtuous life, how is one to cultivate the virtue of patience itself? Are there practices and strategies that help one to become a dispositionally patient person such that patience

1. Feiss, ed., *Monastic Wisdom*, 133.

becomes second nature? How do we recover the habitus of patience for which the early church was renowned?

This is an important question in a culture that encourages a "grass is greener over the fence" restlessness. We often find the grass is *not* greener in another marriage, another church, another house, another vocation, or another geographical location. The pasture on the other side of the fence is often the same hue when we get a closer look, and what we have sought turns out not to satisfy. And it's not just the hue that remains the same; *we* remain the same. Conversion and growth happen when we remain, not when we run—something the ancients associated with the deadly sin of *acedia*. To counter such restlessness, monks are credited with an oft-repeated mantra: "Stay in your cell, and your cell will teach you everything."[2]

This is akin to one of the three vows taken by Benedictine monks—stability, which could be considered a cousin of patience. As mentioned previously, "stability of place" is much like a marriage vow. Monks and couples promise to stay with the same people for the rest of their lives. They may not always be in the same geographical location for various reasons, but like the icon on my GPS, "home" always leads them back to the same community. Stability is premised on the conviction that God places us in *particular* constellations of people so that we can speak to and hear from each other what is needed for our mutual growth into Christlikeness.

But it means more than simply remaining in place. We can live and work with the same people for years without being fully invested in their lives—or in our own. Stability requires attentiveness—paying attention to those with whom we share common space and time. (Recall the importance of attention in the previous chapter.) And this involves persevering in listening, a vital characteristic of the virtue of patience.

2. What is meant by "cell" in these contexts did not preclude frequent visitations among the monks, especially to get advice from older and more experienced monks. See Bunge, *Despondency*, 68.

We need to remain confined to one "cell" of a church or marriage or vocation or geographical location long enough for the depth and richness to take root.[3] Paradoxically, to get somewhere we often need to remain where God has put us. And that is why patience is required. As one scholar of the monastic tradition put it with reference to one of the deadly sins, "In the last analysis, *acedia* [sloth] is flight from God, and it can only be cured by the concrete, patient seeking of God's face. . . . Jesus himself makes this virtue of patience almost an absolute condition for eternal salvation: 'The one who remains steadfast (*hypomone*) will gain life' (Luke 21:19)."[4]

It is the mundane routine of fulfilling the quotidian tasks of everyday existence, following the "schedule," and returning day after day to the same place (such as a workplace) and community (such as a workmate or spouse or family) that provides the specifics for patient endurance.

It is when we attempt to control the situation and the situation does not go as we wish that we are disappointed and slip into despair or cynicism. Mary's response to the angel's announcement about her impending unplanned pregnancy is instructive. To paraphrase: "I don't know what all of this means for my future, but I trust that good things will happen." And so, Mary waited.

In his own way, Robert Roberts affirms what we have said above about stability that combats sloth: Over against the desire to depart from it,

> patience is the ability to dwell gladly in the present moment when we have some desire, or what would be a reason to desire to depart from it. . . . Patience is a form of self-mastery that enables us to dwell in the present moment, to stay in the present task, to narrow our focus of vision so that our mind is not sundered by every passing impulse to quit the present and fly away. . . . Impatience is a constitutionally unpleasant vice. It is a state of more or

3. Of course, this advice does not apply in cases where residence involves abuse or personal endangerment and there is opportunity to move on.

4. Olivera, "Sadness," 359, 369.

> less intense *frustration*: you want to be somewhere other,
> or doing something other, or accomplishing something
> other, or in the company of someone other, than you are.[5]

Roberts gives the example of delaying a race to the local polling location to cast votes before it closed because his son found joy playing
in the puddles on the way. Waiting involves nurturing the moment.

Often it is only when we are patiently present in the moment
that the situation in which God has placed us leads to conversion
and growth in character. As Roberts puts it, patience "gives our
lives continuity and autonomy, enabling us to live not by impulse,
or at the rude beck and call of environmental stimulus, but by
some design."[6] As we alluded to earlier, James implores us at the
beginning of his letter to "*let* endurance have its *full* effect, so that
you may be mature and complete, lacking in nothing" (Jas 1:3–4;
cf. Rom 5:1–5). This is how patience is an active and creative virtue. We exercise patience so that in the end we are saved—in the
fullest sense of salvation, the sense described in Hebrews 10 (vs.
32–39) and 12 (vs. 1–7).

Getting there requires friends who are interested in cultivating this virtue of patience. Mary had Elizabeth—two women who
enabled each other to wait. They affirmed to each other that what
had been promised them was worth waiting for. They made it possible to believe that God was a God who valued life in a world of
dead wombs and pregnant unmarried teens.

So, if the project at hand is acquiring the disposition of patience instead of jumping over the fence, then one must stick to the
project, and there lies the irony: cultivating the virtue of patience
requires patience.

Part of the difficulty in its cultivation, says Michael Casey,
stems from the fact that patience is such a "domestic virtue—the
mundane routine we mentioned earlier: It is not so hard to live
under the delusion that we would rise to the occasion, were heroic
challenges to appear on our horizon. It may be easy for me to believe I would rather die than deny my faith while, at the same time,

5. Roberts, *Strengths of a Christian*, 53–55.
6. Roberts, *Strengths of a Christian*, 55.

mentally murdering a coworker with a booming voice and an empty mind. *Patience concerns how we act in our everyday situations.*"[7]

And Hauerwas and Pinches remind us that every day we have opportunities to cultivate the disposition:

> We have been given time and space for the acquisition of habits that come from worthy activities such as growing food, building shelters, spinning cloth, writing poems, playing baseball, or having children. Such activities not only take time but they create it by forcing us to take first one step and then another. . . . Put simply, our ability to take the time to enjoy God's world, when we are well as when we are sick, depends on our recognition that it is indeed God's world.[8]

The difficulty of the project is exacerbated when we are discouraged by our failures to endure. We practice and practice, yet we seem to be even more prone to be defeated by our impatience. But, again, Hugh Feiss shares wise counsel: "God is patient with us, so we can afford to be patient also. . . . We are saved not by our perfection, but by our identification with the dying and rising of Christ."[9]

A Benedictine monk such as Father Feiss would know about all of this because it is in monastic community that patience is tested and developed. In fact, it should be obvious that qualities such as patience and love and humility can only be developed with practice in community—and hopefully a community of like-minded people engaged in the same moral project. Benedict wrote in his Rule, "This, then, is the good zeal which monks must foster with fervent love: *They should try to be the first to show respect to the other* (Rom 12:10), supporting with the greatest patience one another's weaknesses of body and behavior, and earnestly competing in obedience to one another."[10] Reflecting on this passage, another Benedictine monk, Terrence Kardong, says, "How we bear [one another's weaknesses of body and behavior] says very much about

---

7. Casey, *Balaam's Donkey*, 315, emphasis added.

8. Hauerwas and Pinches, "Practicing Patience," 176–77.

9. Feiss, ed., *Monastic Wisdom*, 134.

10. Fry, ed., *RB1980*, 72.5.

the quality of our life together." It is to be done with patience, one of Benedict's favorite virtues. Reinforced by Benedict's use of the Latin word *patientissime*, which Kardong translates "inexhaustible patience," Kardong affirms: "At any rate, the superlative here must not be watered down, for cenobitic [communal] life is precisely a lifetime exercise in patience."[11]

The Benedictine and first great pope of the church, Gregory the Great, expressed the superlative in his own way with just as much gravitas: "The patient must, therefore, be told to aim *diligently* at loving those whom they must put up with," because when Paul said that love is patient he added that it is kind, "surely showing that those whom it puts up with patiently, it also loves with *unceasing* kindness."[12]

It is true—patience is a divine gift, but it must be cultivated in our interactions with one another (Col 3:12; 2 Tim 4:2), and by our tutelage under the example of others. As Cornelius Plantinga put it so well, "We can apprentice ourselves to patient people. Learning patience is just like learning a musical instrument. You need a good teacher or two. And then you need to practice."[13]

So what strategies can we embodied, communal beings utilize to develop the disposition of patience, especially if a disposition is an acquired habitual response—something like second nature? And what is needed to take it to the superlative level of *inexhaustible* patience, particularly when we are in the irritating company of others?

First, we must gain some self-knowledge and monitor the patterns of impatience from past episodes. What triggers our impatience? Are there certain people, issues, or situations that set us off? If we know the triggers and patterns, then we will not be ambushed. We might even keep a journal reflecting on times when we have become impatient. We will be ready for the next bit of flint that strikes the tinder of impatience so that we can keep the spark from igniting a fire.

11. Kardong, *Benedict's Rule*, 592.

12. Gregory, *Pastoral Care*, 110, emphasis added.

13. Plantinga, *Wings of God*, 56.

But not only must we know ourselves, we must also want to know the other. For instance, in cases where we are inclined to become impatient with another human being (such as following a slowpoke in the freeway's fast lane or wondering when the person in front of us will actually recognize the light has changed to green) we can consider the person with empathy, even when our knowledge of the person is limited to the fact that he or she is an irritant. One psychological technique for such an empathetic response is "cognitive reappraisal" or "reframing"—reinterpreting an event. A person might say to herself, "That driver plodding along or seeming not to pay attention to a traffic signal may have his mind on a family member who is desperately ill, or perhaps she was just fired from her employment, or maybe it's just a case of exhaustion after an eight-hour shift as a cashier in a grocery store with customers who flunked the class on courtesy." By anticipating the trigger and reframing the situation, we can enlarge her heart and treat the other with patience.[14]

And that widened heart can be further extended by memories of the times that others have been patient with us in similar situations. Once when I was not yet a trained and licensed driver I wanted to move one car out of our sloped driveway to make space for a neighborhood whiffle ball game. I took off the emergency brake and steered the car into the back fender of the other family car that had been parked in the driveway. After I went inside and told my father, he came out to inspect the damage. Thinking my allowance might be applied to the cost of repairs for the rest of my home residency, he simply said, "Well, son, I hope this is the worst accident you ever have." It wasn't, but the demonstration of his patience came to mind when our son misjudged a parking situation and scraped a Cadillac with our minivan. Memory of an incident that had occurred more than three decades earlier was what I needed to make a similarly patient response to my son (though his minor scrape was also not the worst accident *he* would have).

But memory does not have to do simply with our personal narratives. It also has to do with the biblical narrative. We must

14. See Mallick and McCandless, "Study of Catharsis," 591, 596.

remember the story into which we have been baptized—the story we truly inhabit. Alan Kreider tells us that catechists in the early church "made it a priority to present the catechumens the Bible's narrative, which would replace the pagan stories as their primary fund of memory." To illustrate, Tertullian's treatise on patience urges his readers to respond nonviolently to attacks, but he knows that it will be difficult for them to live the life of Christian patience and it will strain their new life of learned virtue. When that would happen Tertullian told them to draw on biblical passages they had memorized, such as Jesus' teachings about turning the other cheek.[15]

Tertullian, Cyprian, and Augustine all cited exemplary patience in biblical characters. Job is the proverbial paradigm of the many in Scripture who exhibit patience as passive submission or courageous resistance when faced with suffering or delayed gratification. James (5:11) specifically calls out Job when applauding the *hypomone* of those who endured suffering. Along with Isaiah and the first Christian martyr, Stephen, Tertullian names Job as the exemplar of spiritual and bodily patience.[16]

Tertullian seems especially enamored with Abraham, whose patience *proved* his faith in the incident with Isaac. He was blessed because he was faithful, but he was faithful because he was patient.[17]

Augustine mentions David in the short account (2 Sam 16:5–14) of Shimei, a man of Saul's family, who shadowed David and his men, hurling curses, stones, and dust until the king and his people "arrived weary at the Jordan." David suggested that the Lord might repay him with good for patiently bearing Shimei's cursing. But Augustine is also impressed with Christ's admonition not to prematurely uproot weeds among the kingdom's wheat (Matt 13:24–30), an admonition that may account for Jesus' patient response to

---

15. Kreider, *Patient Ferment*, 157–58. In a footnote (n. 107), Kreider cites Everett Ferguson's claim that "there is ample evidence . . . that the teachings of Jesus on love for enemies and nonretaliation were central to early Christian moral catechesis."

16. Tertullian, "Patience," 14. See Augustine, "Patience," 9.

17. Tertullian, "Patience," 6.

Judas (Matthew 26:49). Augustine cites these as examples of those who maintain a mental patience, while martyrs practice patience with both body and mind.[18]

Cyprian's list adds Abel (one "patiently slain"), Jacob, and Joseph to those already mentioned above. These Old Testament examples "preserved patience with a strong and steadfast equanimity. . . . For the crown of sorrows and sufferings cannot be received unless patience in sorrow and suffering precede it."[19]

With regard to Joseph, I recall a sermon delivered by Diogenes Allen narrating Joseph's story, and years later what I remembered from the sermon he refers to in his autobiographical memoir: "I think the most poignant words in the story are simply 'two years later' that begin chapter 41." Allen imagines Joseph waking each morning hoping to be remembered, to get some good news. But he did not give up hope, which would have been the natural response. He kept praying.[20] "Two years later"—three powerful words that memorialize a patient disposition.

And when we get to the New Testament, Kenneth Bailey is no doubt correct that Mary is the "primary biblical example" of *hypomone*, "standing silently at the cross and choosing not to run away."[21]

In previous chapters we highlighted some contemporary examples of patience. In that vein, another strategy recommended to early catechumens involved imitating role models. As Kreider put it, "They learned to be Christians by watching believers whom they admired." He cites Cyprian's instruction by the example of Caecilianus, from the time of his baptism to his martyrdom. Kreider surmises, "Imitation of this sort must have continued in many places where the master-apprentice relationship was a normal part of the catechetical process."[22]

---

18. Augustine, "Patience," 8.
19. Cyprian, "Patience," 486–87.
20. Allen, *Steps Along the Way*, 62.
21. Bailey, *Jesus*, 389.
22. Kreider, *Patient Ferment*, 159.

Of course, the most significant one to bear in mind when it comes to imitation is the crucified Christ (Heb 12:1–3), particularly if it reaches the heroic level of turning the other cheek or going the extra mile.

Strategies for acquiring patience lead us back to our discussion of faith, hope, and love. For instance, I must exercise faith in God's governance of the world and that must include a robust hope that divine governance will assure the fruitful result of patience. Curtis Almquist, a monk of St. John of the Cross in Massachusetts, reminds us that "waiting figures prominently in creation," in which plants, animals, night and day all "follow a cadence that resists being rushed." Even with our efforts to fight a pandemic, "We still face an element of waiting for what is beyond our ultimate control." This is difficult. It is a "quality of suffering" that entails "dependence, exposure, being no longer in control of your own situation, being the object of what is done." But such circumstances are "an invitation for patience" that may turn out to be "a time of gestation for new life beyond what you could have imagined."[23]

It is in this context that Hauerwas and Pinches make a perceptive observation: "As a society, nothing upsets us more than having to wait for our bodies." If we have not cultivated the virtue of patience *before* we are sick, we will not have the patience required *when* we are sick. Our sick bodies do not allow us to do whatever we want, so that this "given" can afford us an opportunity to practice patience in a way that teaches us we are not our own creations: "Put simply, our ability to take the time to enjoy God's world, when we are well as when we are sick, depends on our recognition that it is indeed God's world."[24] This is something I am having to learn as a former runner, now with osteoarthritis of the hip. Though I haven't quite mastered the required patience, waiting for my body now means walking instead of running.

As mentioned before, Hugh Feiss develops this reminder that we are not always in control of our own situation in the context of accepting those injustices that are unavoidable. There are times

23. Almquist, "Waiting," lines 6–7, 12–13, 15–16, 21, 25.
24. Hauerwas and Pinches, "Practicing Patience," 166, 176–77.

when we are obliged to respond aggressively. And then there are other times when we must bear persecution for the sake of justice, keeping in mind that patience produces character (James 1:4). In those times, we must remember that such patience is a gift of a loving God who seeks our perfection—our resemblance to Christ.

Augustine discusses this *gift* of patience that comes from the Holy Spirit over against a Pelagian suggestion that it can be had by our own free will, and this is borne out by the object of our love. Augustine asks how we are to understand those who bear patience without the aid of God. He answers that the greater the love of God in saints, "the more do they endure all things for Him whom they love," so that patience is the result. But those who have a greater "lust of the world, the more do they endure all things for that which they lust after," so that a false patience is the result. False patience suffers for what one lusts after, while true patience (human will divinely aided by the Holy Spirit) endures all for the love of God. Of course, for Augustine, only one who has been *first* chosen and loved can choose or love with such patience. But his point is that there cannot be true patience in us apart from the love of God that endures all things. It is the case that false patience is motivated by "deceitful visions and unclean incentives" that end up demonstrating a "marvelous endurance of intolerable evils." But a good will given by God that loves God and neighbor will endure *all* things. Even those who do not deny Christ but break from the church possess a patience to be praised as they suffer "tribulations, straits, hunger, nakedness, persecution, perils, prisons, bonds, torments, swords, or flames, or wild beasts, or the very cross, through fear of hell and everlasting fire." Ultimately, Augustine argues that even the "poor of Christ" will patiently bear suffering because they know that God "will put no end to everlasting happiness, who gives patience to the will for the time being: because both the eternal happiness and the temporal patience is given by God as a gift heaped on our love, and our love itself is a gift of God."[25]

But this gift of patience that is grounded in the love of God requires effort to *abide* in Christ's love, rather than drowning in

25. Augustine, "Patience," 12–26.

a sea of distractions and difficulties that foster impatience. God's love is made visible in Christ, and maintaining awareness and acceptance of such divine love requires the practice of prayer and immersion in the Word, especially when we are tempted to neglect such practices and seal ourselves off in self-sufficiency. It must be cultivated in bodily practices, as Tertullian reminded his readers that Christ exhibited patience bodily. For example, he suggests that imitating Christ in the "bodily patience" of fasting "adds a grace to our prayers for good, a strength to our prayers against evil; this opens the ears of Christ *our* God, dissipates harshness, elicits compassion." Patience is "she who is entrusted by holiness with the care of sexual purity" [for the widow, the virgin, the eunuch]. For Tertullian, patience must be translated from the mind to the body: "it is true that the ruling mind easily communicates the gifts of the Spirit with its *bodily* habitation. . . . That which springs from a virtue of the *mind* is perfected in the *flesh*; and, finally, by the patience of the flesh, does battle under persecution" as in cases involving imprisonment, whippings, fire, crucifixion, beasts, and sword. "When, however, it is led forth unto the final proof of happiness, unto the occasion of the second baptism [i.e., martyrdom], unto the act of ascending the divine seat, no patience is more needed *there* than *bodily* patience."[26]

The one thing we should not do is to defend ourselves against impatience by escaping or by blaming others. John Cassian warned monks not to defend their impatience by secluding themselves in their cells or settling into the remote desert:

> Let us not, then, look for our peace without, or think that another's patience can mitigate the vice of our own impatience. For, just as the kingdom of God is within us, so also "a person's enemies are those of his own household," because no one is more opposed to me than my own disposition, which truly is the most intimate part of my household. Therefore, if we are careful, we shall be unable to be troubled by internal enemies, for where those of our own household are not opposed to us, there

26. Tertullian, "Patience," 13, italics in the original.

also the kingdom of God is attained in tranquility of mind. . . . I shall not be able to be troubled by anyone, however malicious he may be, if I do not fight against myself with a turbulent heart. But if I am hurt, it is not the fault of another's attack but of my own impatience.[27]

In the end, we are motivated by the knowledge that patience is necessary for happiness, while impatience is accompanied by unhappiness (the "I can't wait until . . ." mental state). This is why patience is not simply "teeth-gritting endurance" or suppression.

The person who has developed the *disposition* of patience knows this. Think of an activity you so enjoy doing that you would stick to it in such a way that it would not make sense to say you were patiently enduring it. In the same way, a person who has cultivated the disposition of patience will *look like* the one enjoying the activity even when the patiently disposed person encounters a situation or activity about which we would normally be impatient.

I began this book with a warning situated in a population of average adults who *are* normally impatient when it comes to reading. Perhaps reading this book has provided practice in the cultivation of patience, though hopefully it has not been an experience of teeth-gritting endurance. It at least afforded an opportunity to *listen*. Patience is required for listening. Listening is one of the hallmarks of the patient person, particularly in a noisy world that is filled with manifestations of impatience—hasty remarks, thoughtless retorts, mindless pontifications.

So, if nothing else comes of what you have read, hopefully when you put this book on the shelf, you have the patience to listen to the sister or brother in community, to listen to the cries of those who wait for justice, to listen to the voice in your head that suggests a fellow commuter may have good reasons for the way the driver is maneuvering, and to listen for the voice of God who may or may not be speaking right now. It's a beginning on the way to the cultivation of the creative activity of patience.

27. Cassian, *Conferences*, 18.15.

Bibliography

Allen, Diogenes. *Steps Along the Way: A Spiritual Autobiography*. New York: Church Publishing, 2002.

Almquist, Curtis. "Waiting, So Difficult and So Promising." https://www.ssje. org/2020/05/13/waiting-so-difficult-and-so-promising/.

Augustine. "On Patience." In *St. Augustine: On the Holy Trinity, Doctrinal Treatises, Moral Treatises*, edited by Philip Schaff, translated by H. Browne, vol. III, *A Select Library of the Nicene and Post-Nicene Fathers of the Christian Church*, 1st series, 527–36. Grand Rapids: Eerdmans, 1988.

Bailey, Kenneth. *Jesus Through Middle Eastern Eyes*. Downers Grove, IL: InterVarsity, 2008.

Barth, Karl. *Church Dogmatics II/1: The Doctrine of God*, edited by G. W. Bromiley and T. F. Torrance. Translated by T. H. L. Parker et al. Edinburgh: T. & T. Clark, 1957.

———. *Church Dogmatics III/1: The Doctrine of Creation*, edited by G. W. Bromiley and T. F. Torrance. Translated by J. W. Edwards. Edinburgh: T. & T. Clark, 1958.

Berger, Eric. *The US Constitution through History*. Chantilly, VA: The Teaching Company, 2022.

Billings, Todd. *The End of the Christian Life: How Embracing Our Mortality Frees us to Truly Live*. Grand Rapids: Brazos, 2020.

Bloesch, Donald. *The Paradox of Holiness*. Peabody, MA: Hendrickson Academic, 2016.

———. *The Pursuit of Holiness*. Peabody, MA: Hendrickson Academic, 2016.

———. *Spirituality Old & New*. Downers Grove, IL: InterVarsity, 2007.

Branch, Taylor. *Parting the Waters: America in the King Years 1854–63*. New York: Simon and Schuster, 1988.

Bunge, Gabriel. *Despondency: The Spiritual Teaching of Evagrius Ponticus on Acedia*. Yonkers, NY: St. Vladimir's Seminary Press, 2012.

Caird, G. B. *A Commentary on the Revelation of St. John the Divine*. New York: Harper & Row, 1966.

Casey, Michael. *Balaam's Donkey: Random Ruminations for Every Day of the Year*. Collegeville, MN: Liturgical, 2019.

———. *A Guide to Living in the Truth: Saint Benedict's Teaching on Humility*. Liguori, MO: Liguori/Triumph, 2001.

Cassian, John. *The Conferences*. Translated by Boniface Ramsey. New York: Paulist, 1997.

Coles, Robert. *The Story of Ruby Bridges*. Jefferson City, MO: Scholastic, 1995.

Cyprian. "Treatise IX: On the Advantage of Patience." In *Hippolytus, Cyprian, Caius, Novatian*, edited by Alexander Roberts and James Donaldson, vol. V of *The Ante-Nicene Fathers: The Writings of the Fathers down to A.D. 325*, 484–91. Grand Rapids: Eerdmans, 1990.

Dozeman, Thomas B. "Patience." In *The Westminster Theological Wordbook of the Bible*, edited by Donald E. Gowan, 353–54. Louisville: Westminster John Knox, 2003.

Ellsberg, Robert, ed. *The Duty of Delight: The Diaries of Dorothy Day*. Milwaukee: Marquette University Press, 2008.

Ellul, Jacques. *The Technological Society*. New York: Vintage, 1964.

Fagenberg, David W. "Time in the Desert Fathers." *American Benedictine Review* 50.2 (June 1999) 180–202.

Falkenroth, U., and C. Brown. "Patience, Steadfastness, Endurance" (*anechomai*). In *The New International Dictionary of New Testament Theology*, vol. 2., edited by Lothar Coenen, Erich Beyreuther, and Hans Bietenhard, 764–66. Grand Rapids: Zondervan, 1986.

Feiss, Hugh. *Essential Monastic Wisdom: Writings on the Contemplative Life*. San Francisco: Harper San Francisco, 1999.

Fitch, Robert. *Of Love and Suffering*. Philadelphia: Westminster, 1970.

Fry, Timothy, ed. *RB1980: The Rule of Benedict in English*. Collegeville, MN: Liturgical, 1981.

Gelles-Watnick, Risa, and Andrew Perrin. "Who Doesn't Read Books in America?" https://www.pewresearch.org/fact-tank/2019/09/26/who-doesnt-read-books-in-america/.

Goldingay, John. *Psalms, Volume 1, Psalms 1–41*. Grand Rapids: Baker Academic, 2006.

———. *Psalms, Volume 3, Psalms 90–150*. Grand Rapids: Baker Academic, 2008.

Gregory the Great. *Pastoral Care*. Translated by Henry Davis. Ancient Christian Writers 11. New York: Newman, 1978.

Hauerwas, Stanley. *Hannah's Child: A Theologian's Memoir*. Grand Rapids: Eerdmans, 2010.

———. *The Peaceable Kingdom: A Primer in Christian Ethics*. Notre Dame: University of Notre Dame Press, 1983.

Hauerwas, Stanley, and Charles Pinches. "Practicing Patience: How Christians Should Be Sick." In *Christians Among the Virtues: Theological Conversations with Ancient and Modern Ethics*, 166–78. Notre Dame: University of Notre Dame Press, 1977.

Bibliography

Hauerwas, Stanley, and Samuel Wells. "The Gift of the Church and the Gifts God Gives It." In *The Blackwell Companion to Christian Ethics*, edited by Stanley Hauerwas and Samuel Wells, 13–27. Oxford: Blackwell, 2006.

Hoezee, Scott. *The Riddle of Grace: Applying Grace to the Christian Life.* Grand Rapids: Eerdmans, 1996.

Hoose, Phillip. *Claudette Colvin: Twice Toward Justice.* New York: Farrar, Straus and Giroux, 2009.

Jan, Julius von. "O Land, Land, Land: Hear the Word of the Lord" In *Preaching in Hitler's Shadow: Sermons of Resistance in the Third Reich*, edited by Dean G. Stroud, 106–14. Grand Rapids: Eerdmans, 2013.

Kardong, Terrence G. *Benedict's Rule: A Translation and Commentary.* Collegeville, MN: Liturgical, 1996.

Kendi, Ibram X. "*Patience* Is a Dirty Word." *The Atlantic*, July 23, 2020. https://www.theatlantic.com/ideas/archive/2020/07/john-lewis-and-danger-gradualism/614512/.

Kreider, Alan. *The Patient Ferment of the Early Church: The Improbable Rise of Christianity in the Roman Empire.* Grand Rapids: Baker Academic, 2016.

Mallick, Shahbaz Khan, and Boyd R. McCandless. "A Study of Catharsis of Aggression." *Journal of Personality and Social Psychology* 4.6 (1966) 591–96.

Mays, John L. *Psalms.* Louisville: John Knox, 1994.

Merton, Thomas. *New Seeds of Contemplation.* New York: New Directions, 1972.

Migliore, Daniel. *Faith Seeking Understanding: An Introduction to Christian Theology.* 3rd ed. Grand Rapids: Eerdmans, 2014.

Mouw, Richard J. *Abraham Kuyper: A Short and Personal Introduction.* Grand Rapids: Eerdmans, 2011.

Nouwen, Henri. *Finding My Way Home.* Chestnut Ridge, NY: Crossroad, 2004.

Ogliari, Donato. "*Laus Patientiae*: Theological, Anthropological and Monastic Facets of Patience." *American Benedictine Review* 45.1 (March 1994) 6–21.

Okholm, Dennis. *Dangerous Passions, Deadly Sins: Learning from the Psychology of Ancient Monks.* Grand Rapids: Brazos, 2014.

Olivera, Bernnardo. "A Sadness That Undermines the Longing for God." *American Benedictine Review* 60.4 (December 2009) 357–70.

Pascal, Blaise. *Pensees.* Translated by W. F. Trotter. New York: Random House, 1941.

Pieper, Josef. *The Four Cardinal Virtues.* Notre Dame: University of Notre Dame Press, 1966.

Plantinga, Cornelius. *Under the Wings of God.* Grand Rapids: Brazos, 2023.

Rahner, Karl. "Why and How Can We Venerate the Saints?" In *Theological Investigations, VIII*, translated by David Bourke, 3–23. New York: Herder & Herder, 1971.

Roberts, Robert C. *Recovering Christian Character: The Psychological Wisdom of Søren Kierkegaard.* Grand Rapids: Eerdmans, 2022.

———. *The Strengths of a Christian.* Philadelphia: Westminster, 1984.

Bibliography

Rutledge, Fleming. *The Crucifixion: Understanding the Death of Jesus Christ.* Grand Rapids: Eerdmans, 2017. "

———. "When God Is Silent." In *Advent: The Once and Future Coming of Jesus Christ*, 115–21. Grand Rapids: Eerdmans, 2018.

Sampson, Anthony. *Mandela: The Authorized Biography.* New York: Vintage, 2000.

Schaff, Philip, ed. *Doctrinal Treatises, Moral Treatises.* Grand Rapids: Eerdmans, 1988.

Schibler, Daniel. "*Qwh.*" In *New International Dictionary of Old Testament Theology & Exegesis*, vol. 3, edited by Willem A. VanGemeren et al., 892–96. Grand Rapids: Zondervan, 1997.

Sider, Ronald J., ed. *The Early Church on Killing: A Comprehensive Sourcebook on War, Abortion, and Capital Punishment.* Grand Rapids: Baker Academic, 2012.

Taylor, Barbara Brown. "The Silence of God." In *God in Pain: Teaching Sermons on Suffering*, 110–14. Nashville: Abingdon, 1998.

Tertullian. "Of Patience." In *Latin Christianity: Its Founder, Tertullian*, edited by Alexander Roberts and James Donaldson, translated by S. Thelwall, vol. III of *The Ante-Nicene Fathers*, 707–18. Grand Rapids: Eerdmans, 1986.

Thielicke, Helmut. *How to Hope Again.* Philadelphia: Fortress, 1970.

Wadell, Paul J. *Becoming Friends: Worship, Justice, and the Practice of Christian Friendship.* Grand Rapids: Brazos, 2002.

Warren, Tish Harrison. *Liturgy of the Ordinary: Sacred Practices in Everyday Life.* Downers Grove, IL: InterVarsity, 2016.

Weil, Simone. *Waiting for God.* Translated by Emma Craufurd. New York: Harper Perennial Modern Classics, 2009.

Wilken, Robert Louis. *The Spirit of Early Christian Thought: Seeking the Face of God.* New Haven: Yale University Press, 2003.

Williams, Rowan. *Anglican Identities.* Lanham, MD: Cowley, 2003.